Your NAME

....

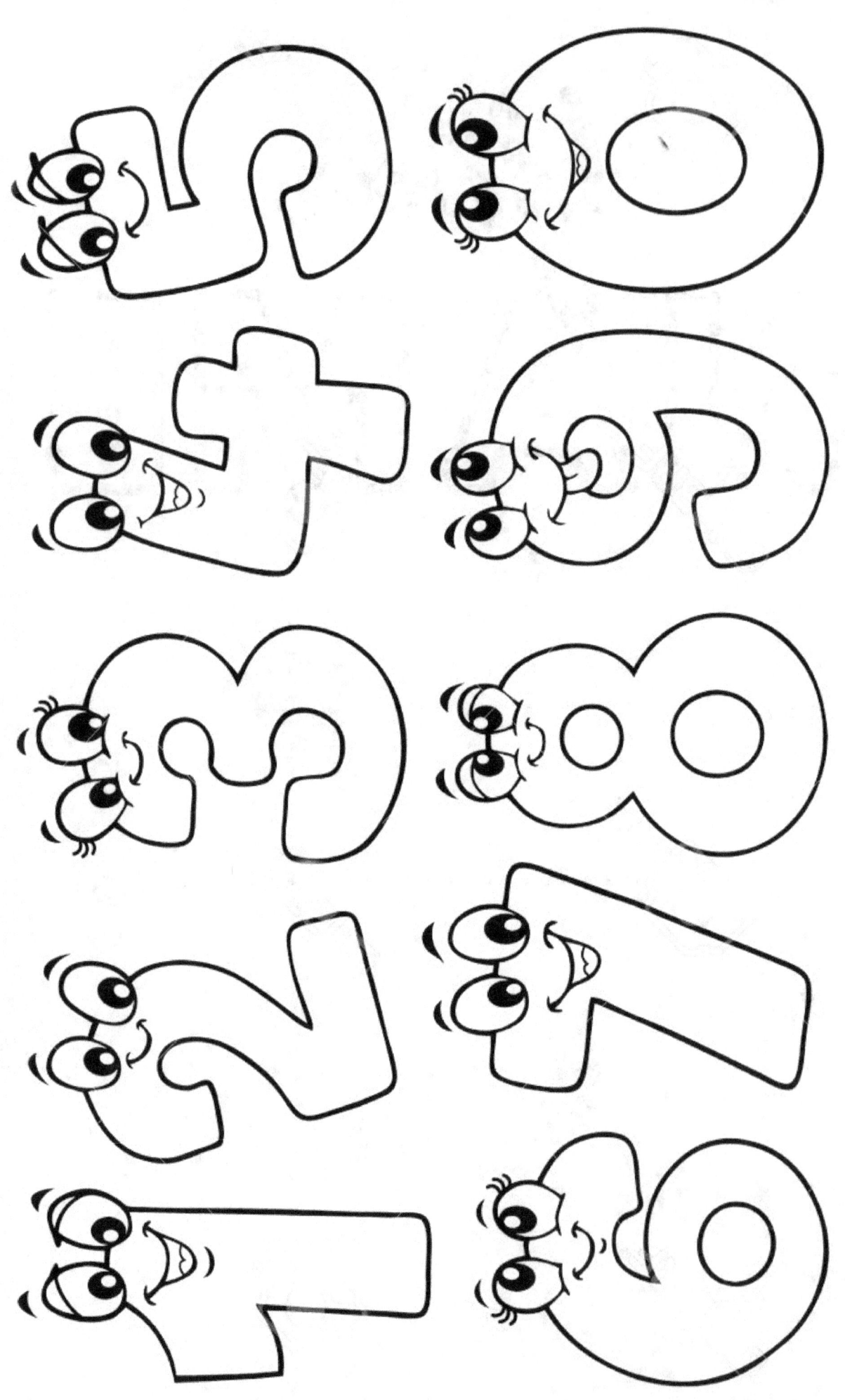

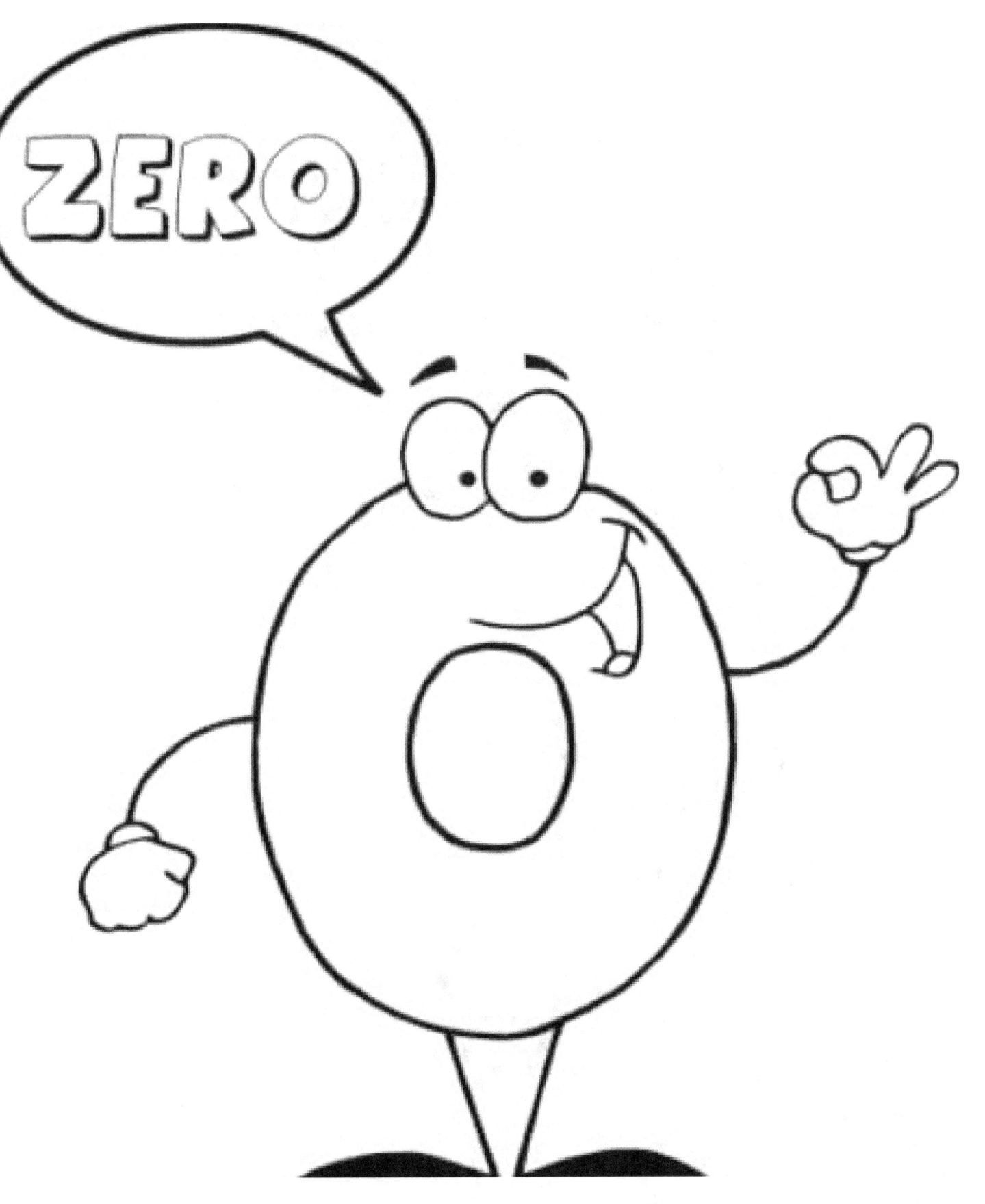

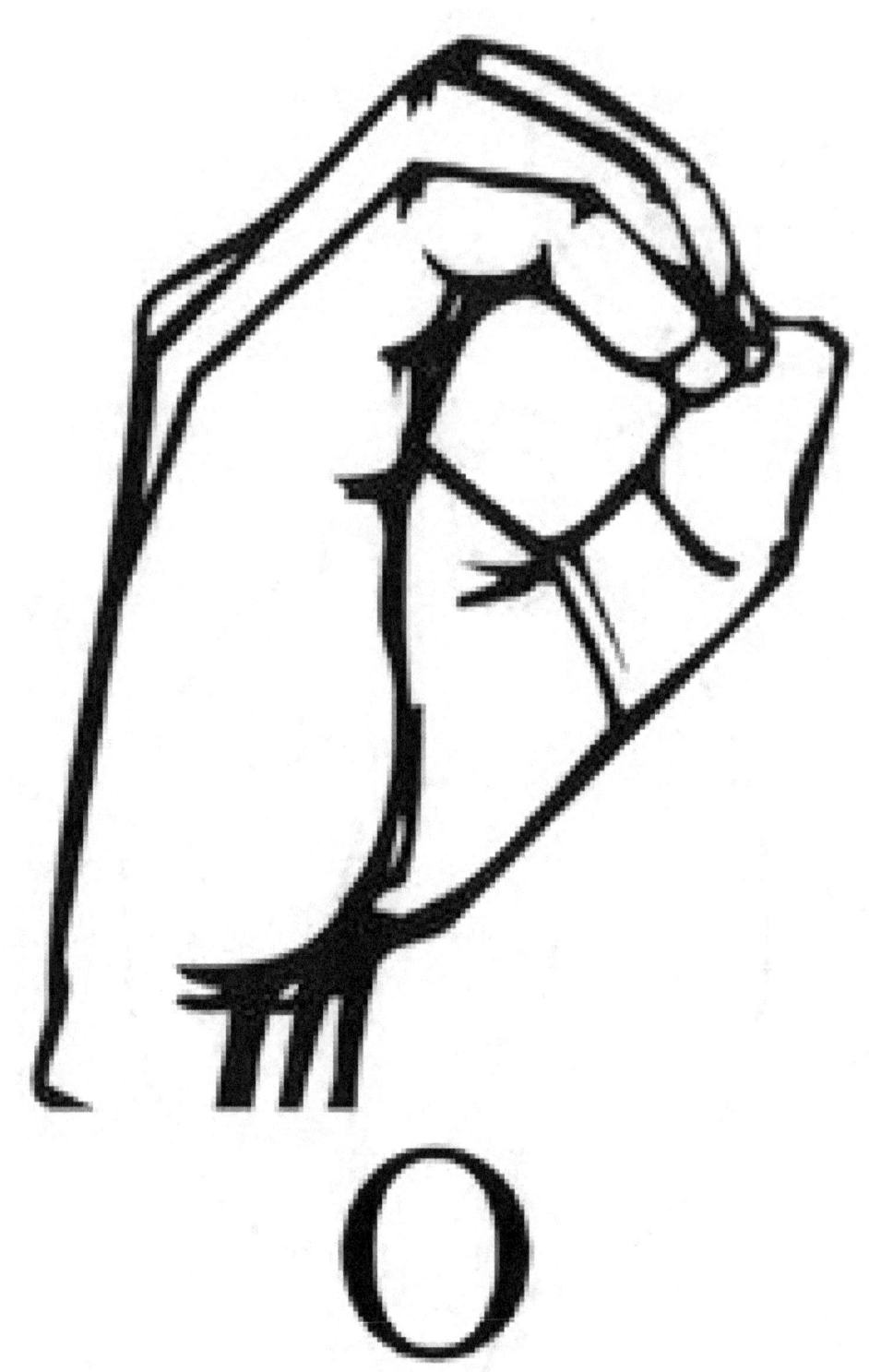

O

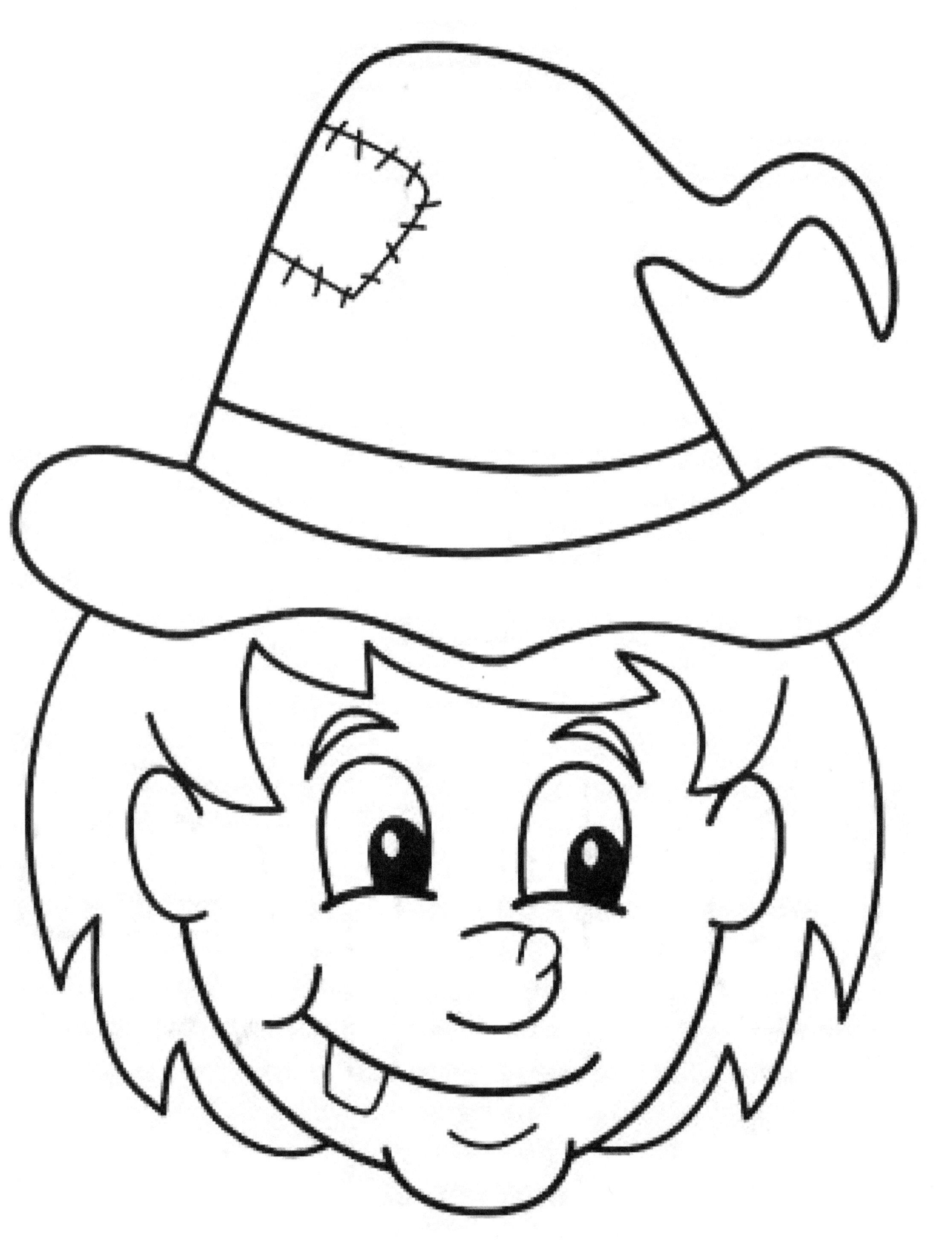

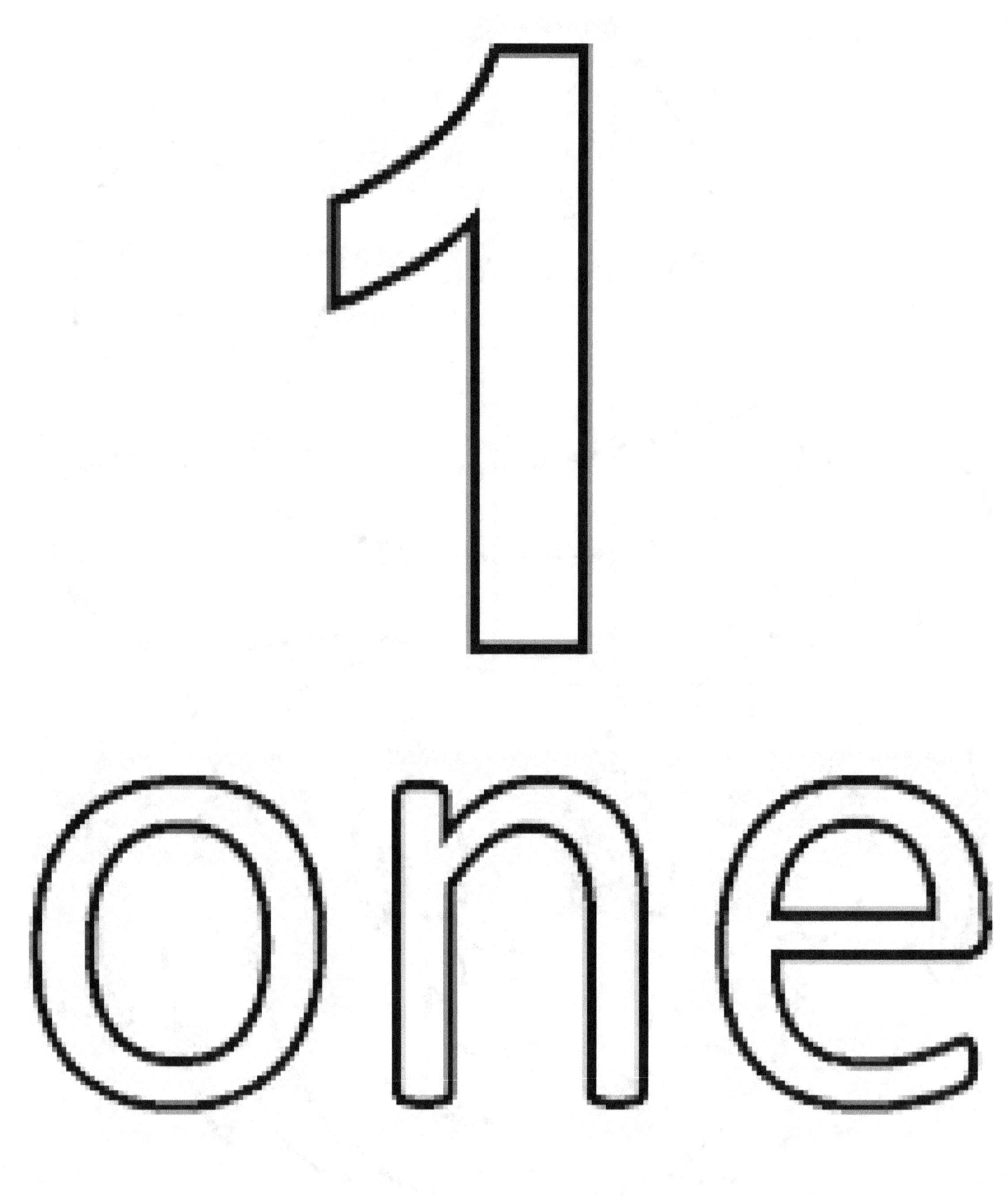

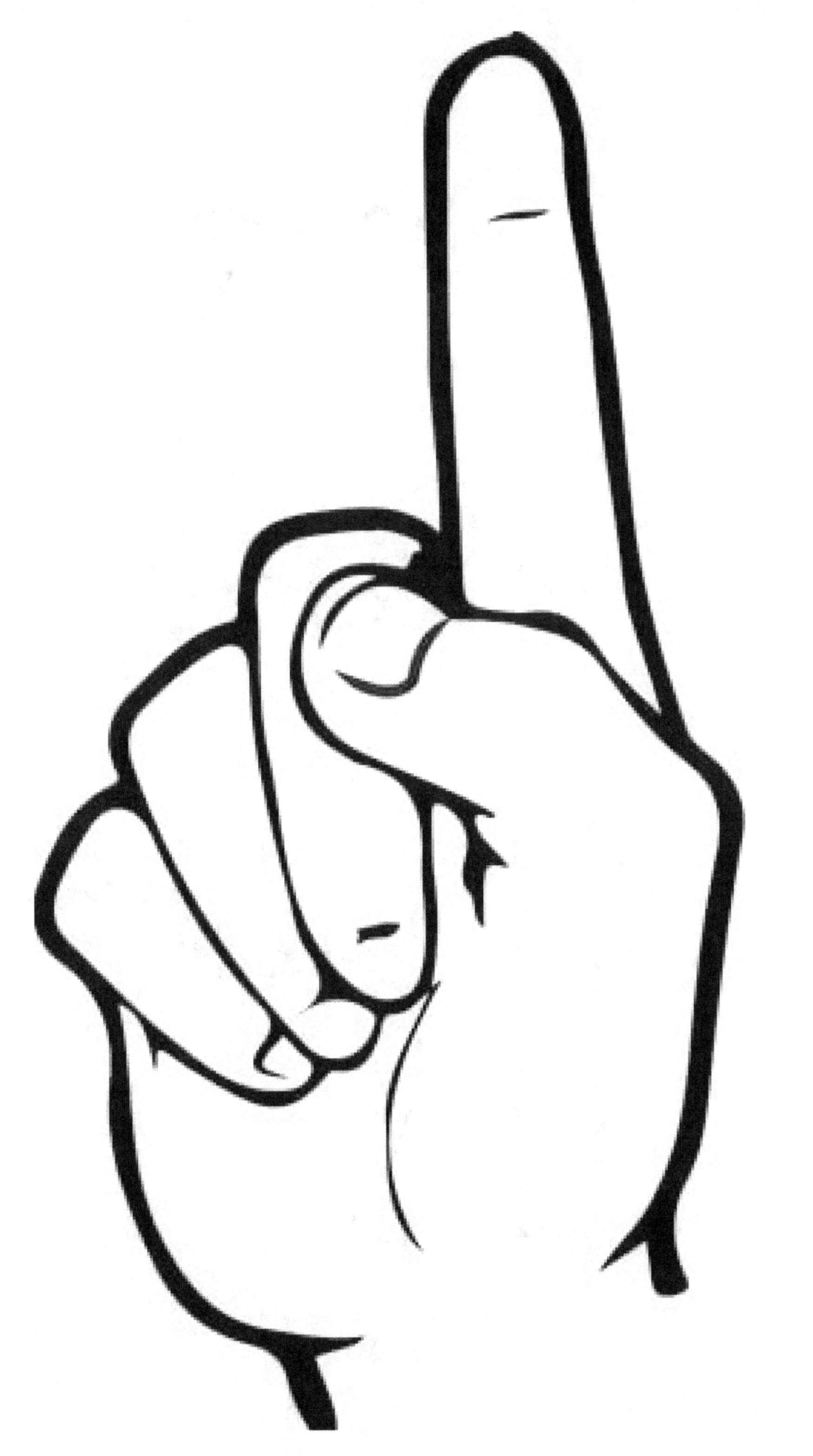

One Apple

1

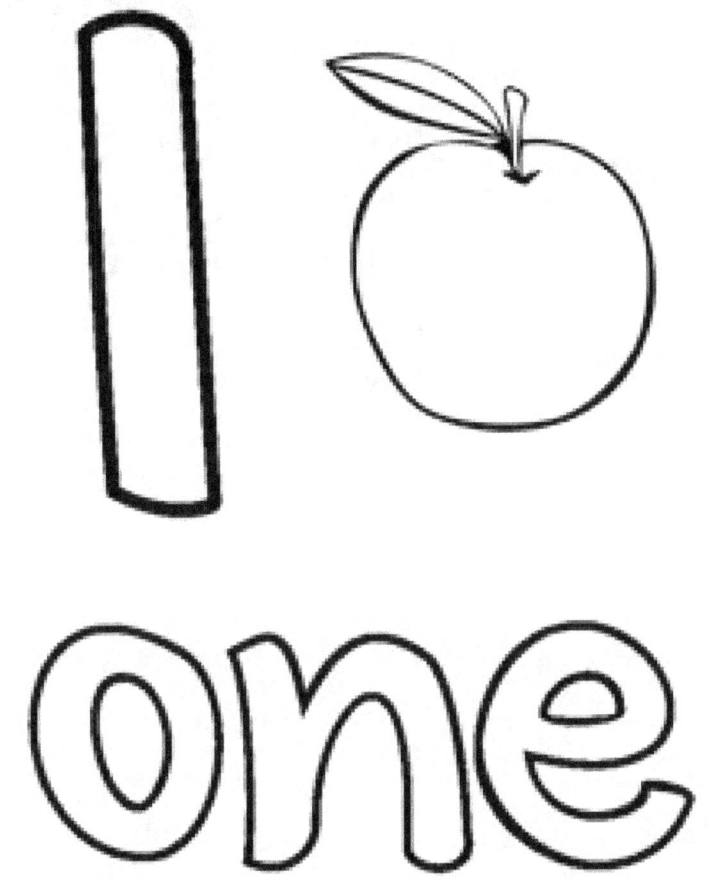

One Apple

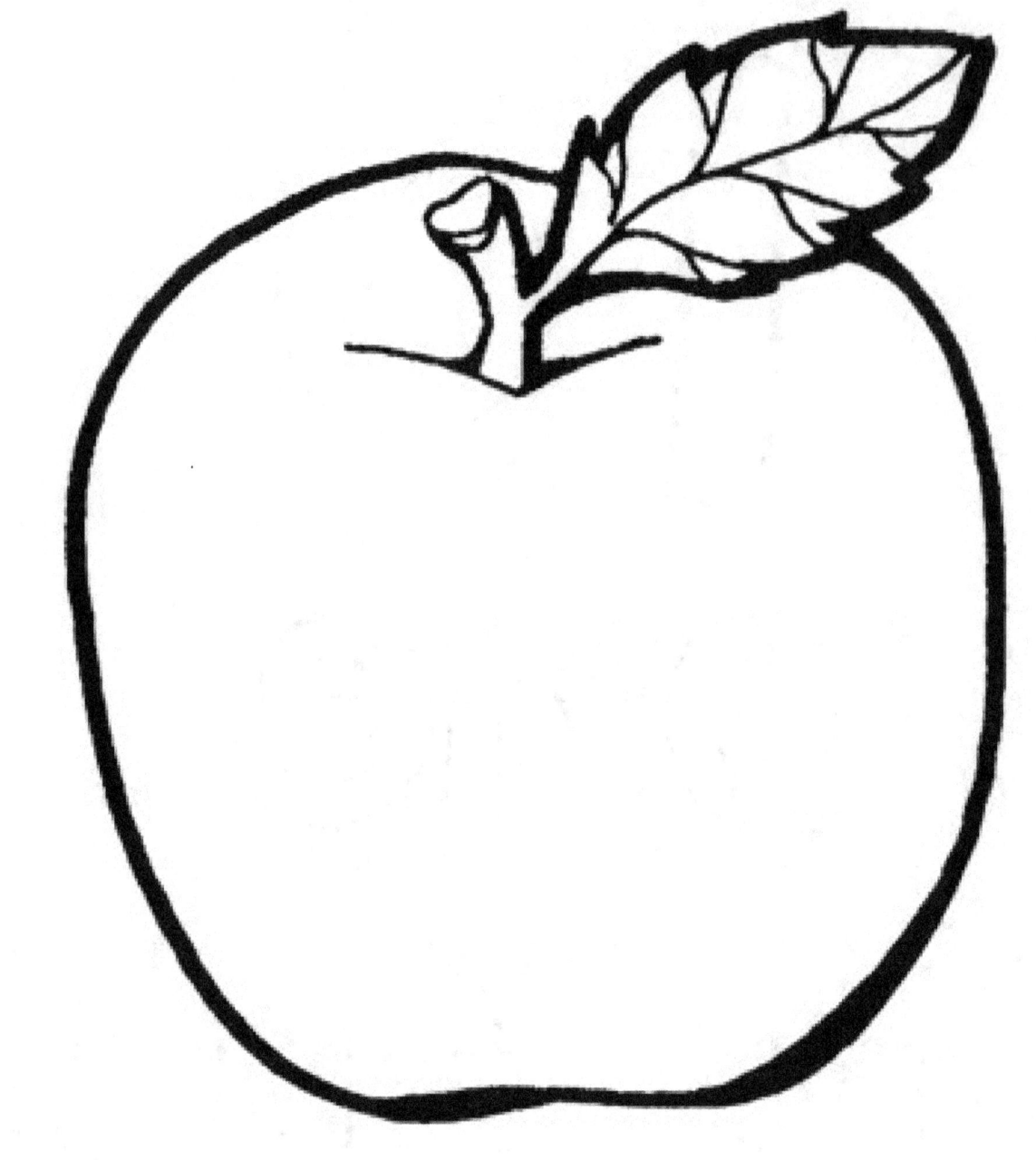

One Red Apple

2
two

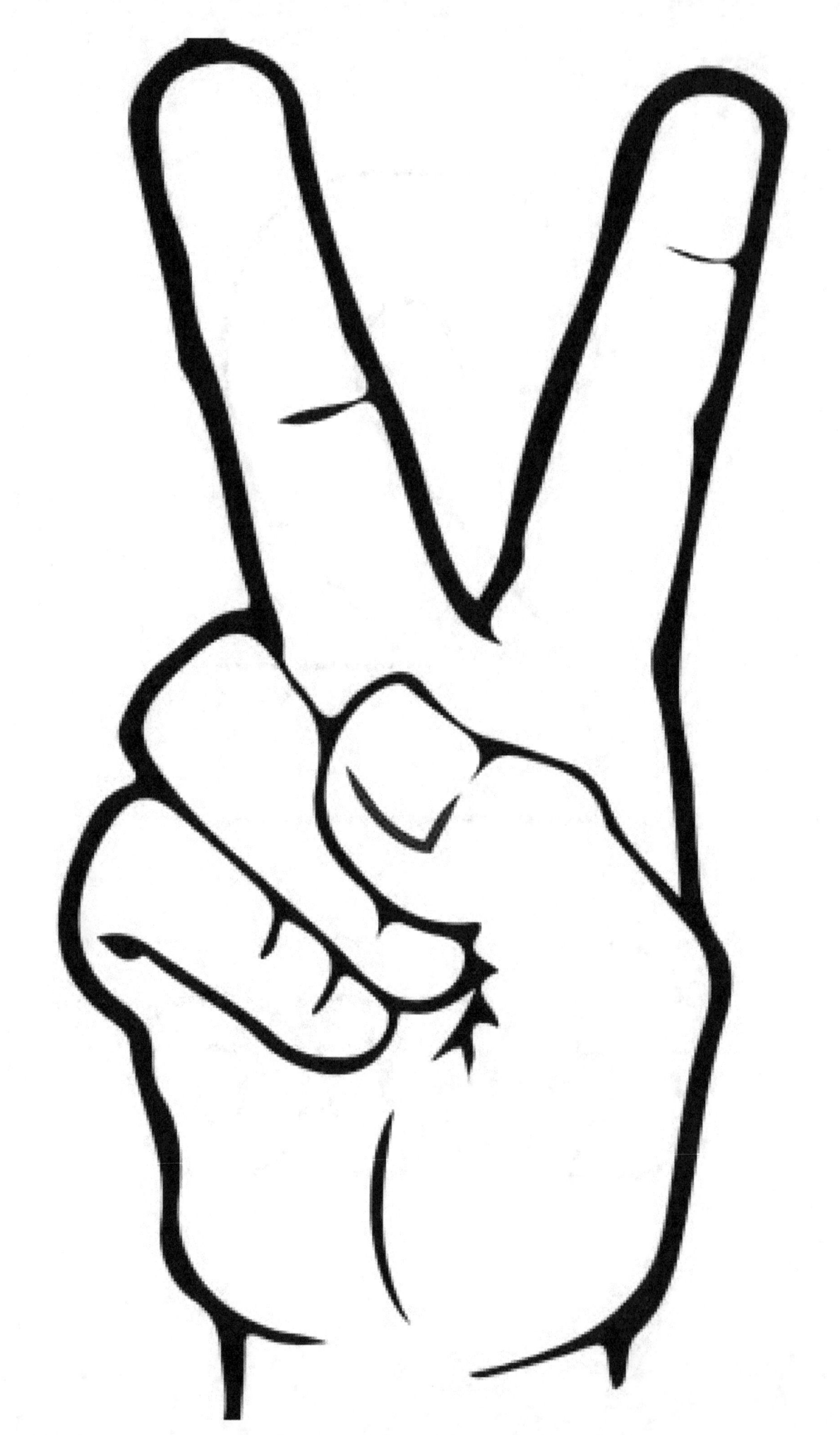

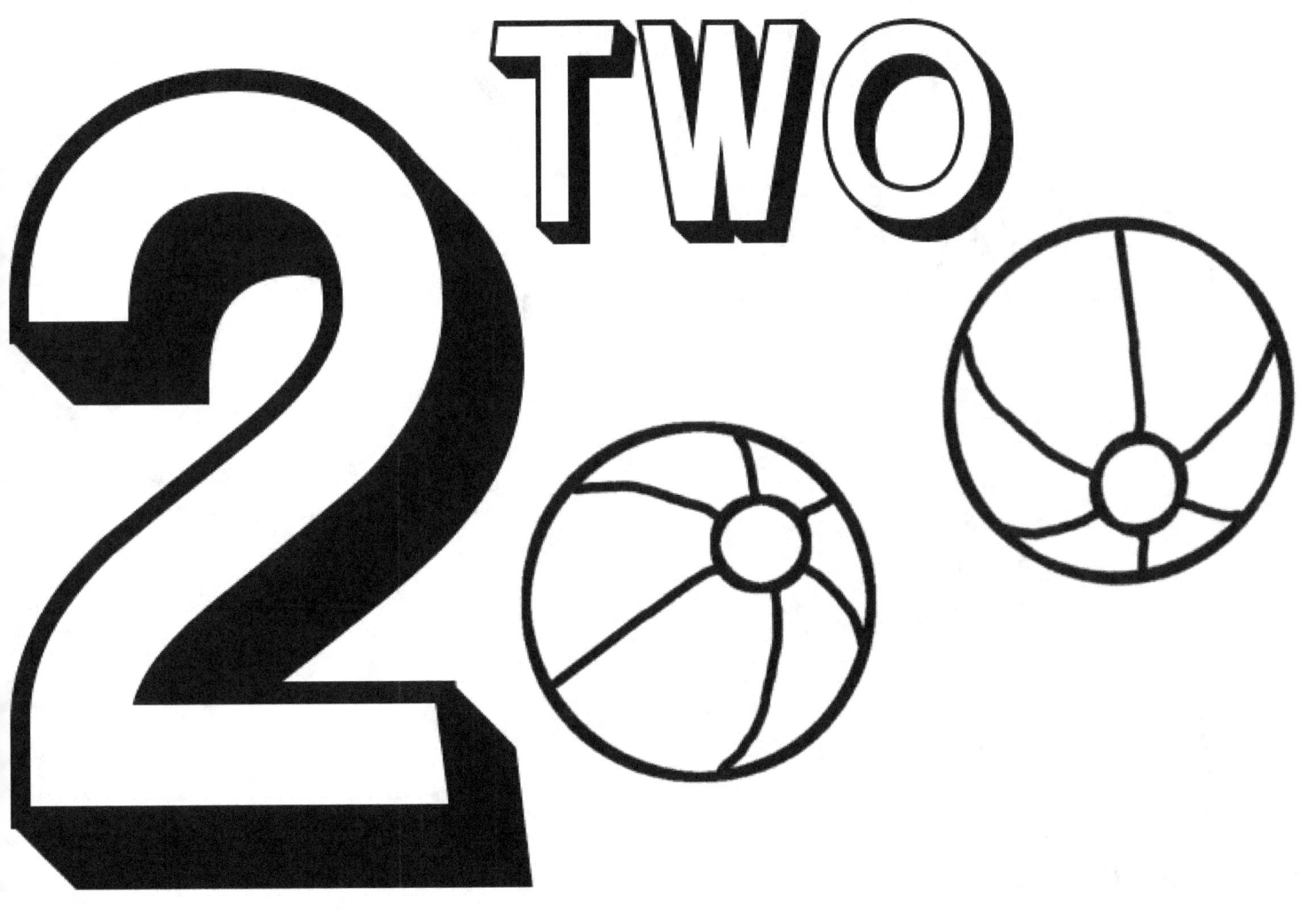

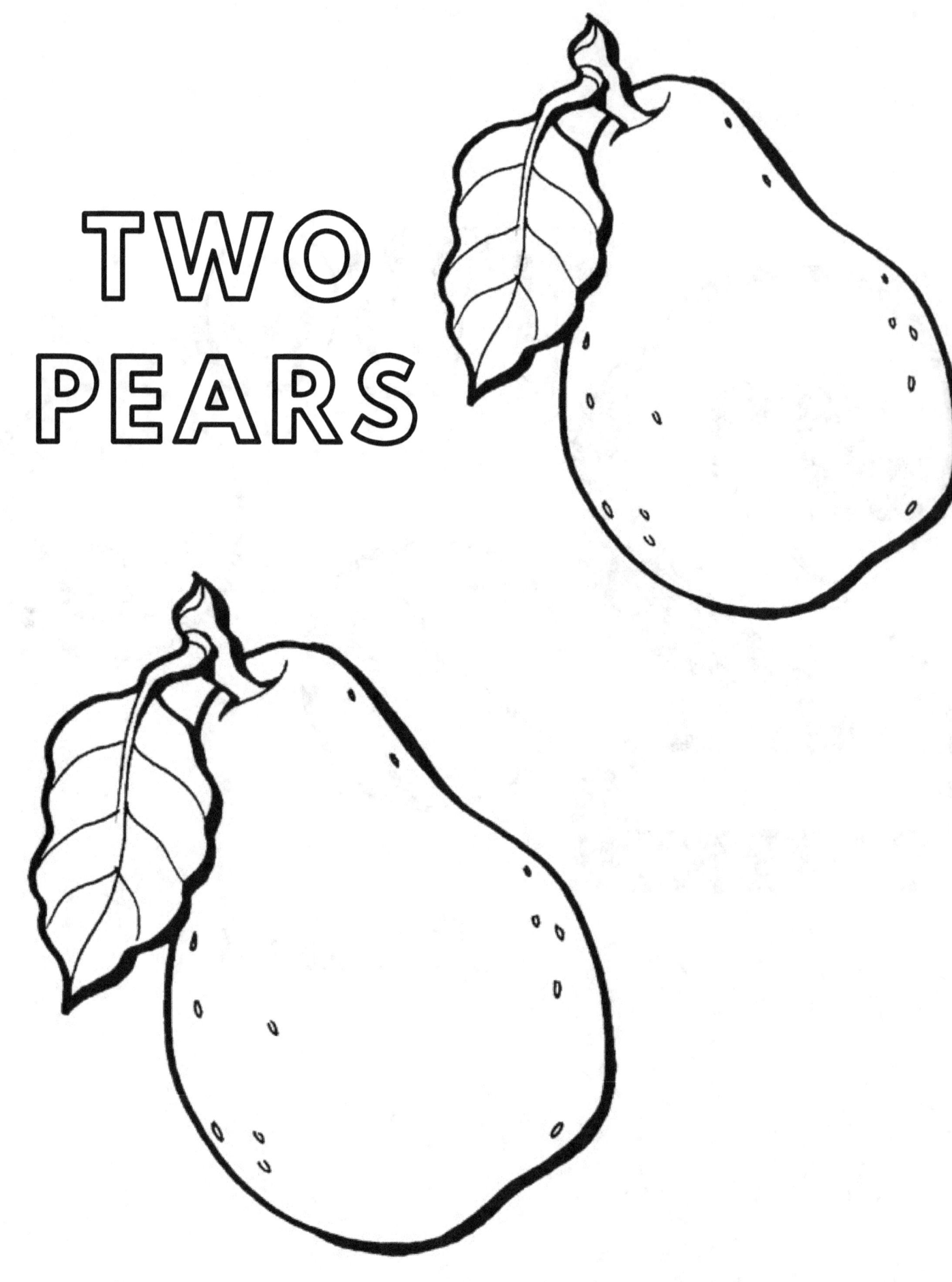

3

three

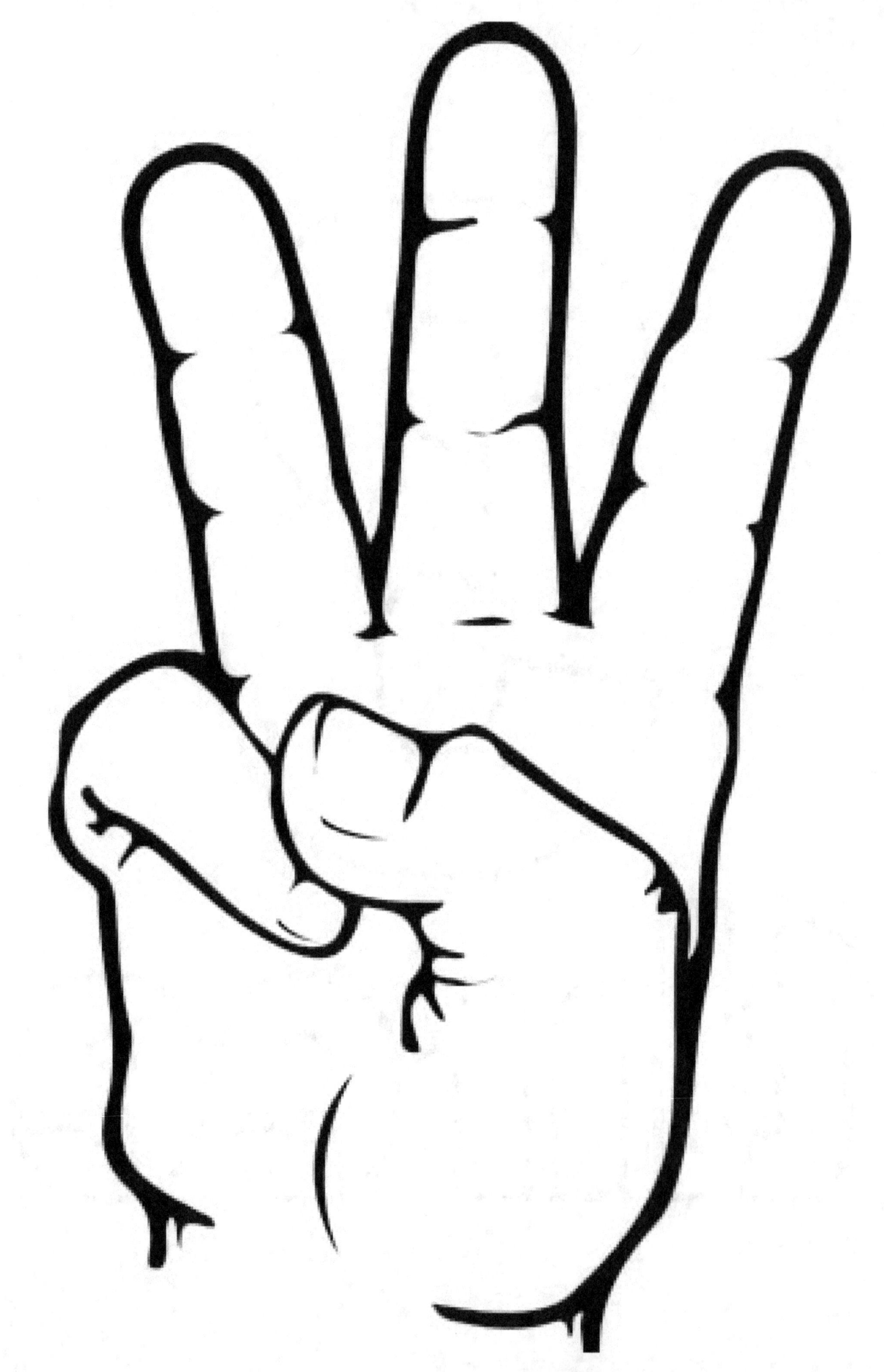

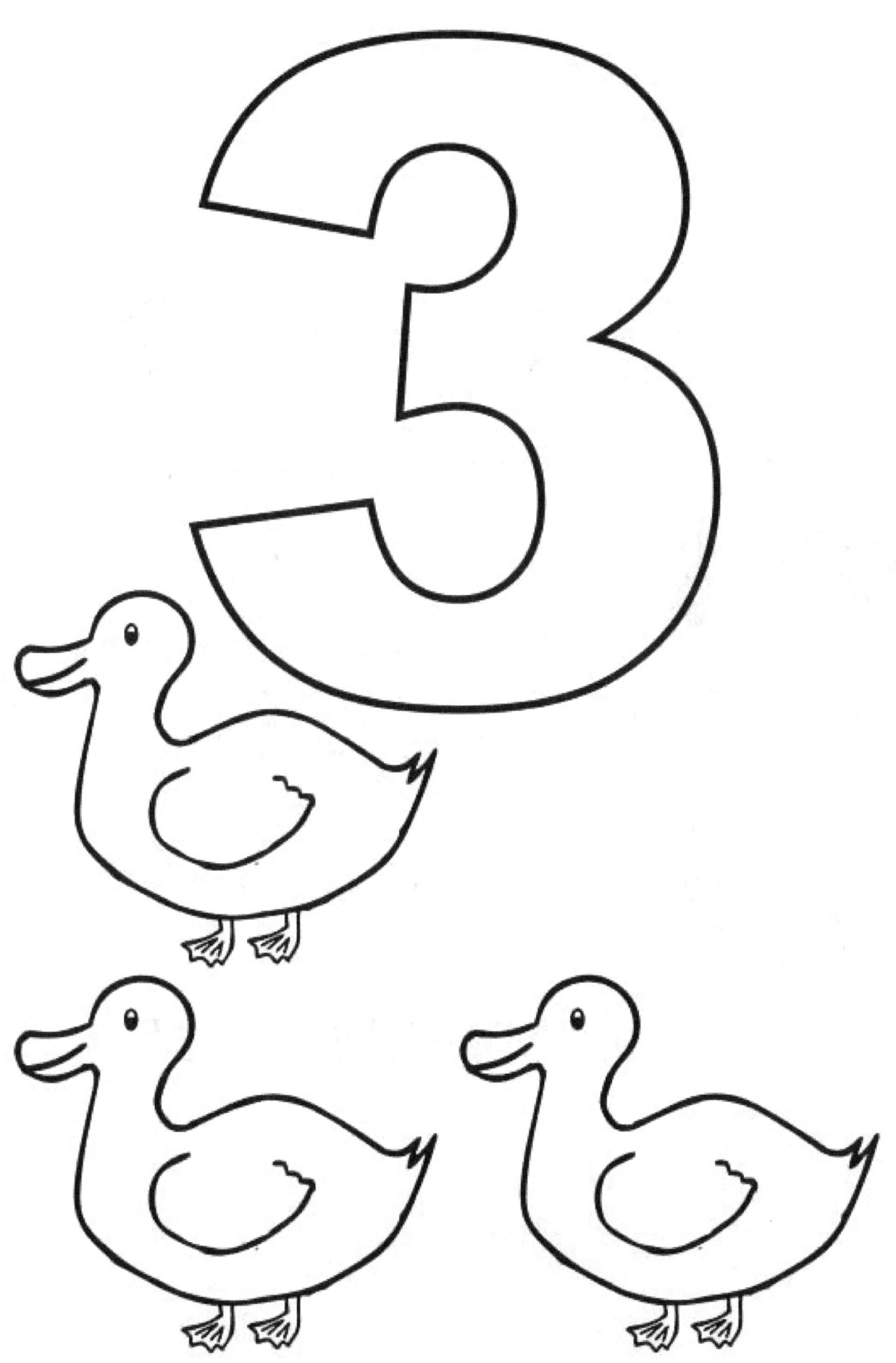

THREE

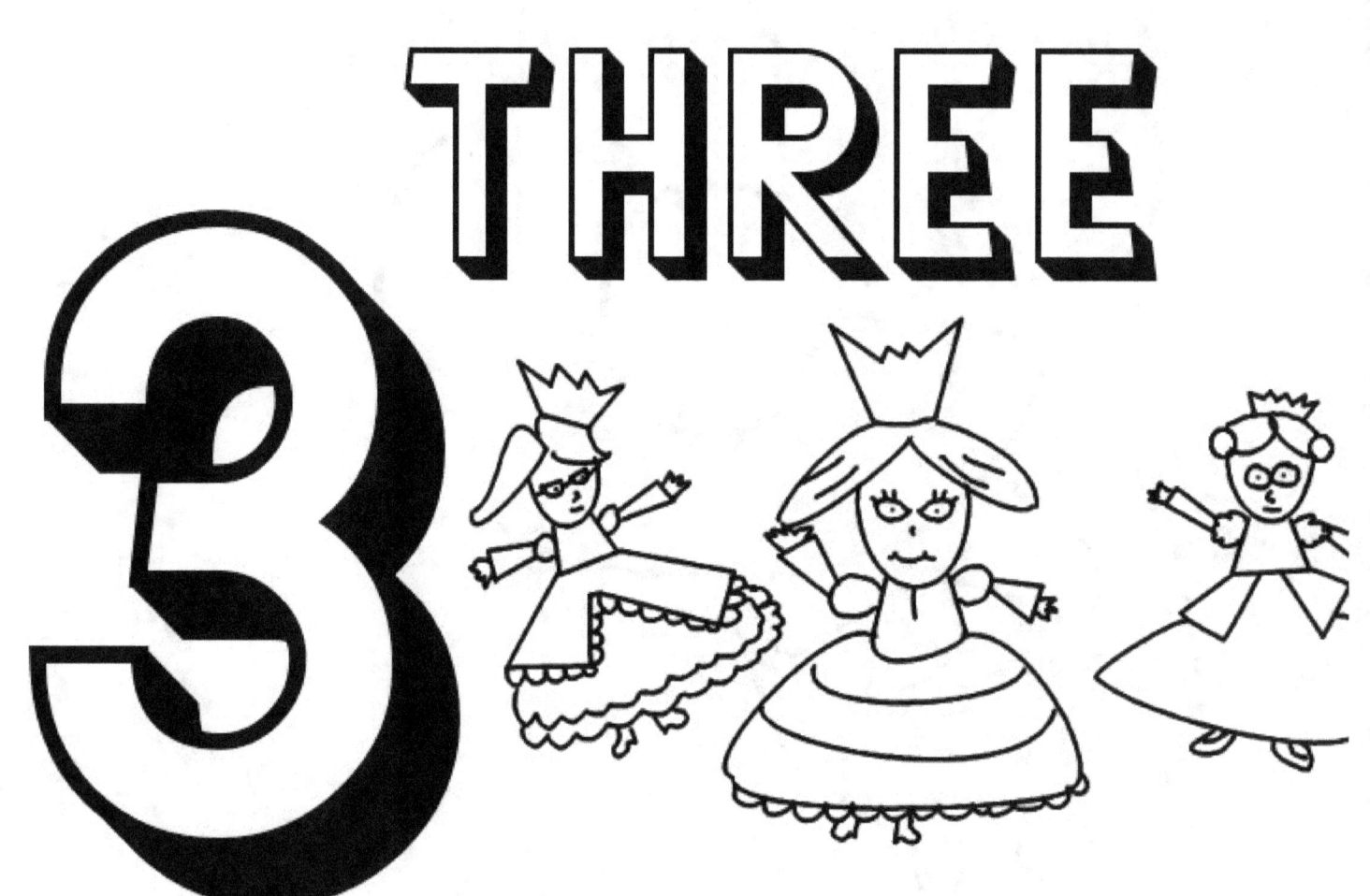

THREE PRINCESSES

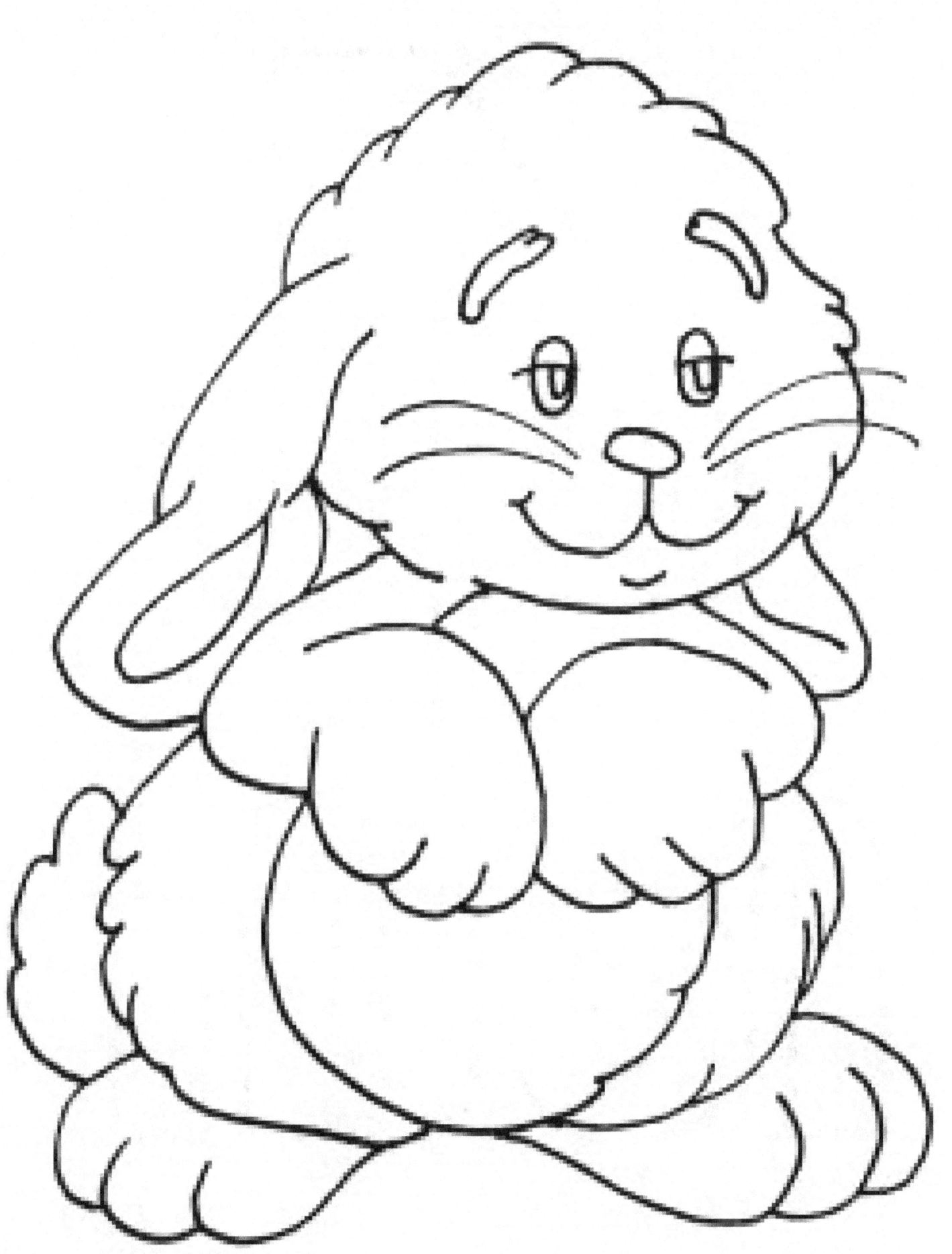

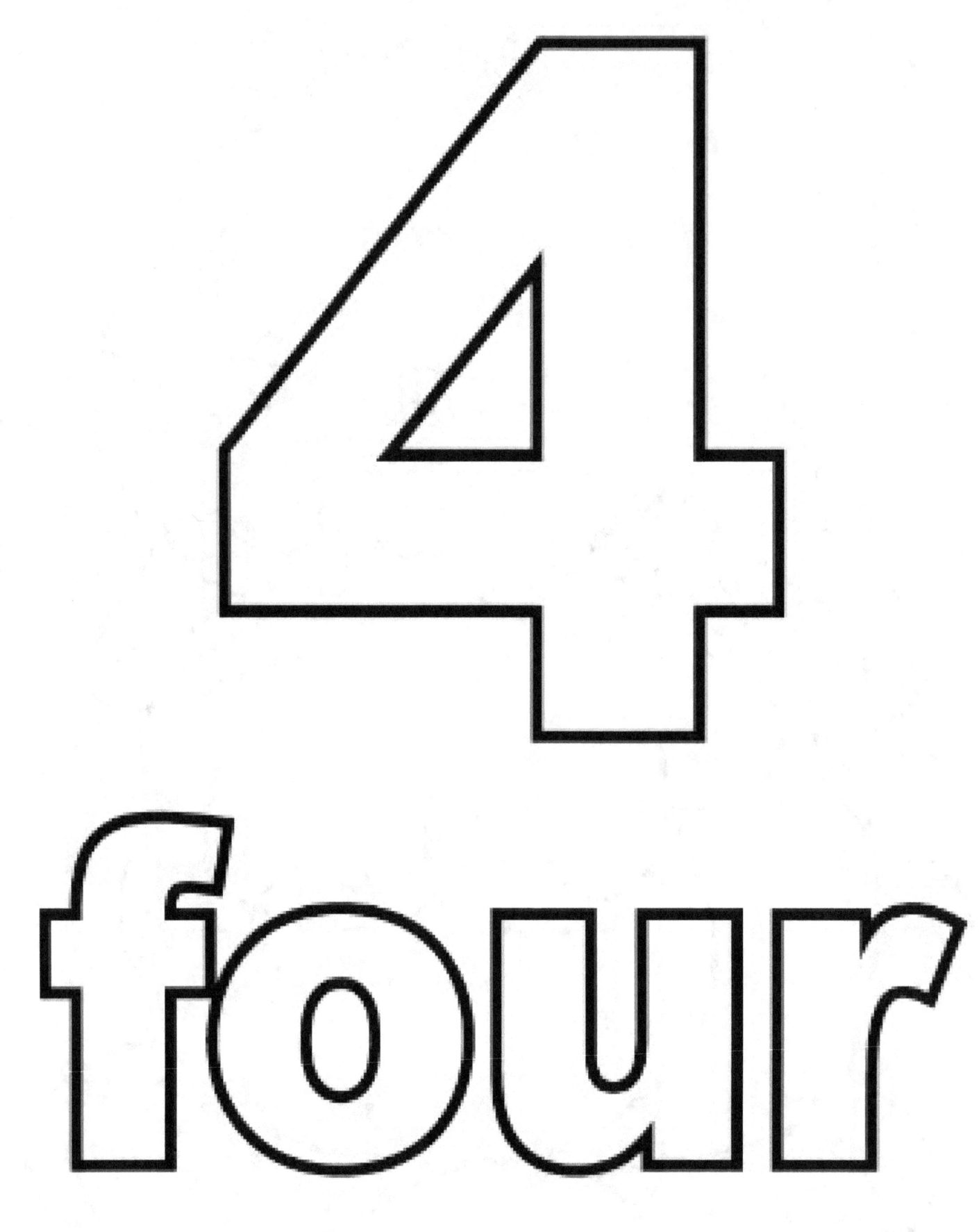

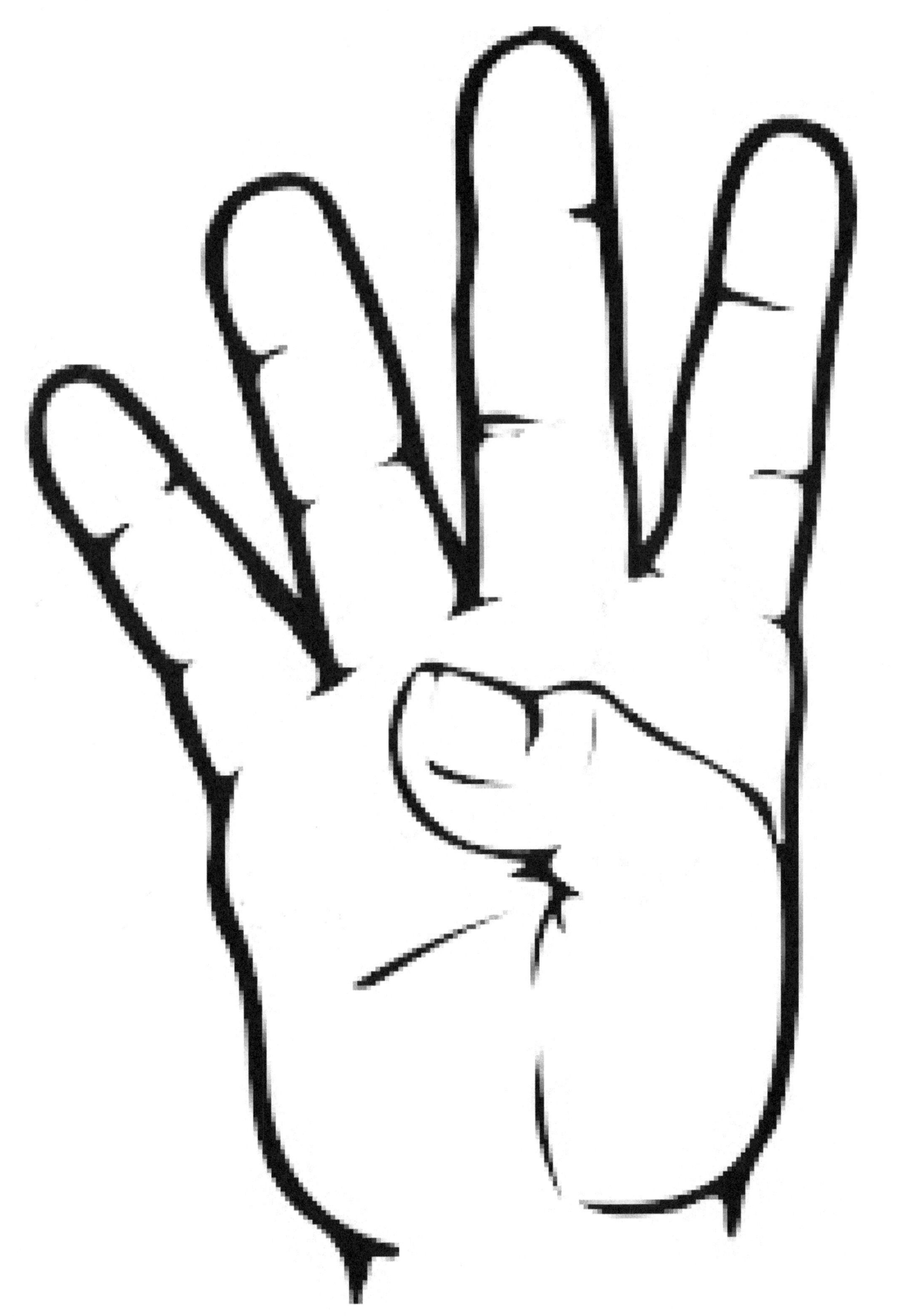

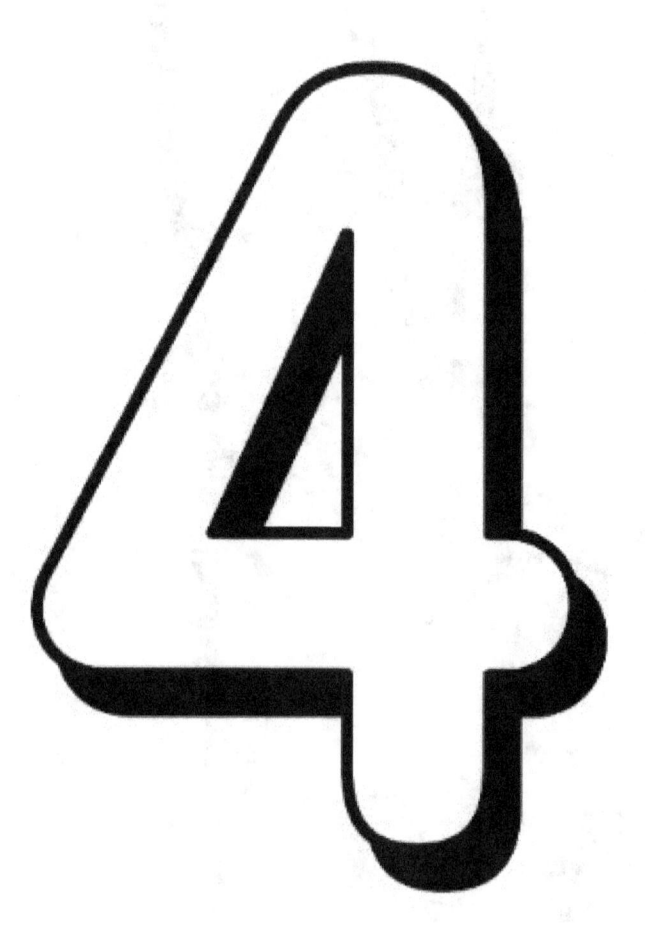 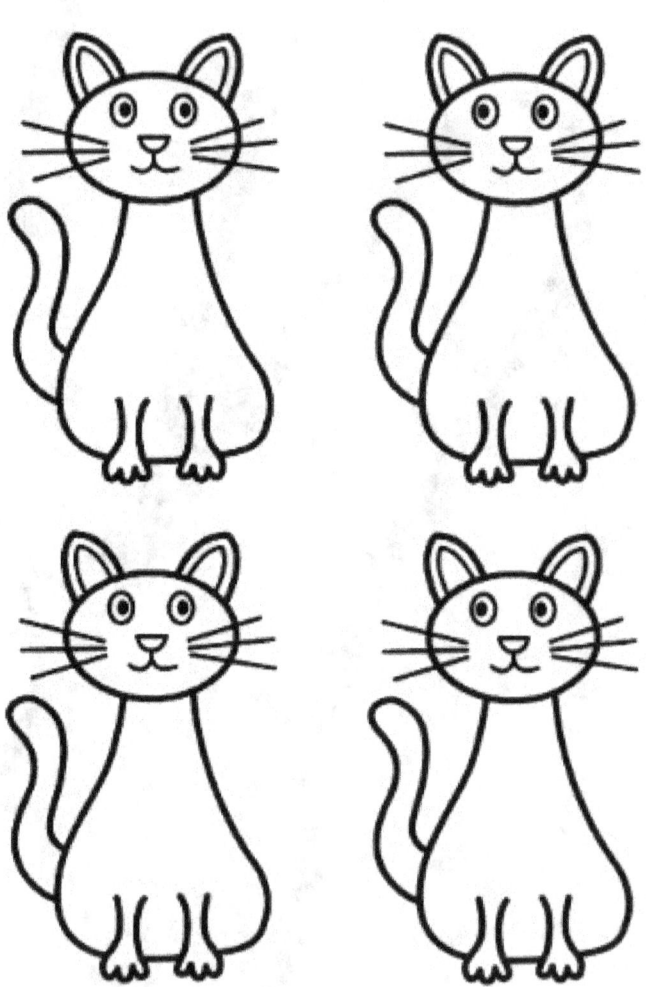

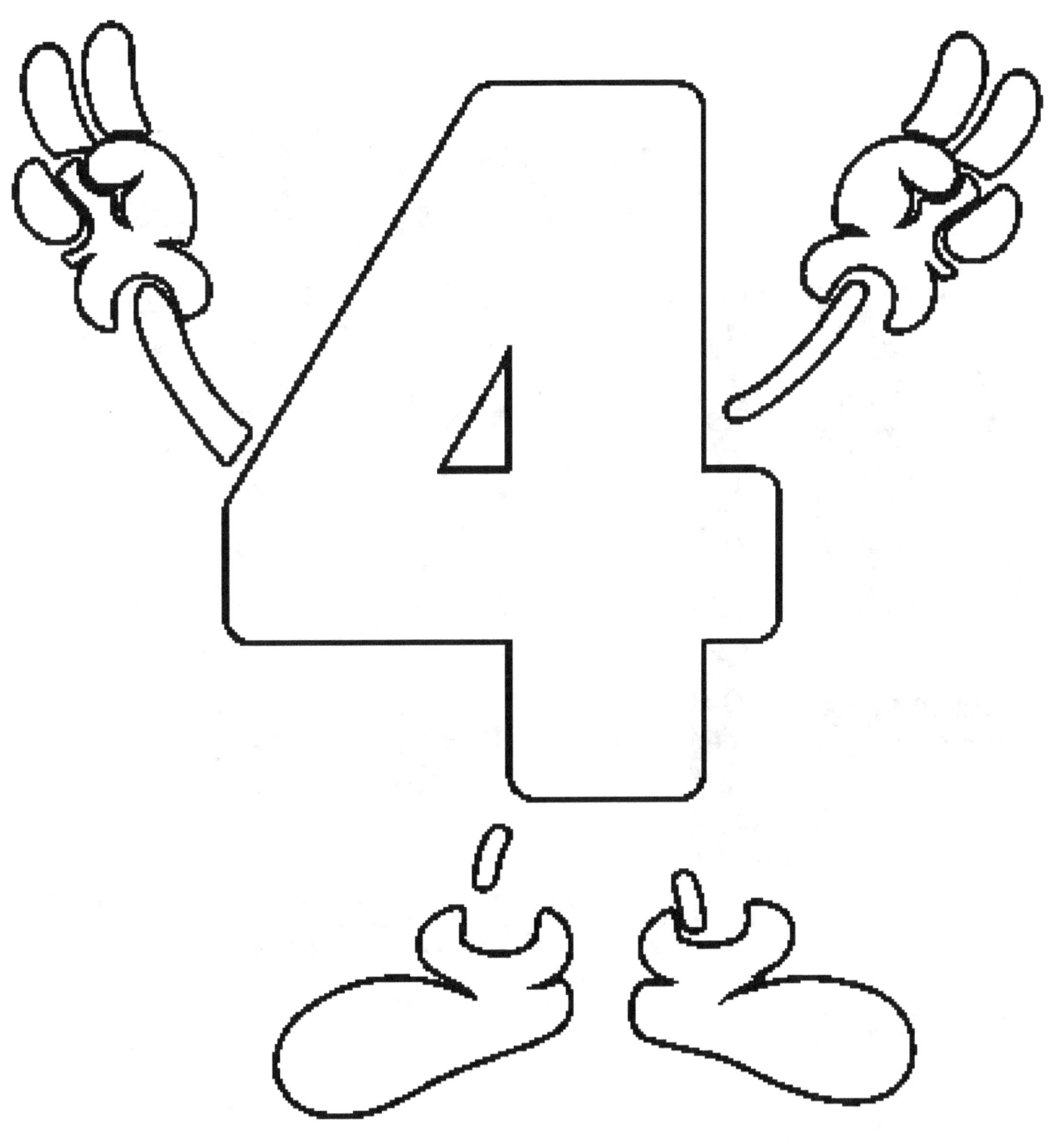

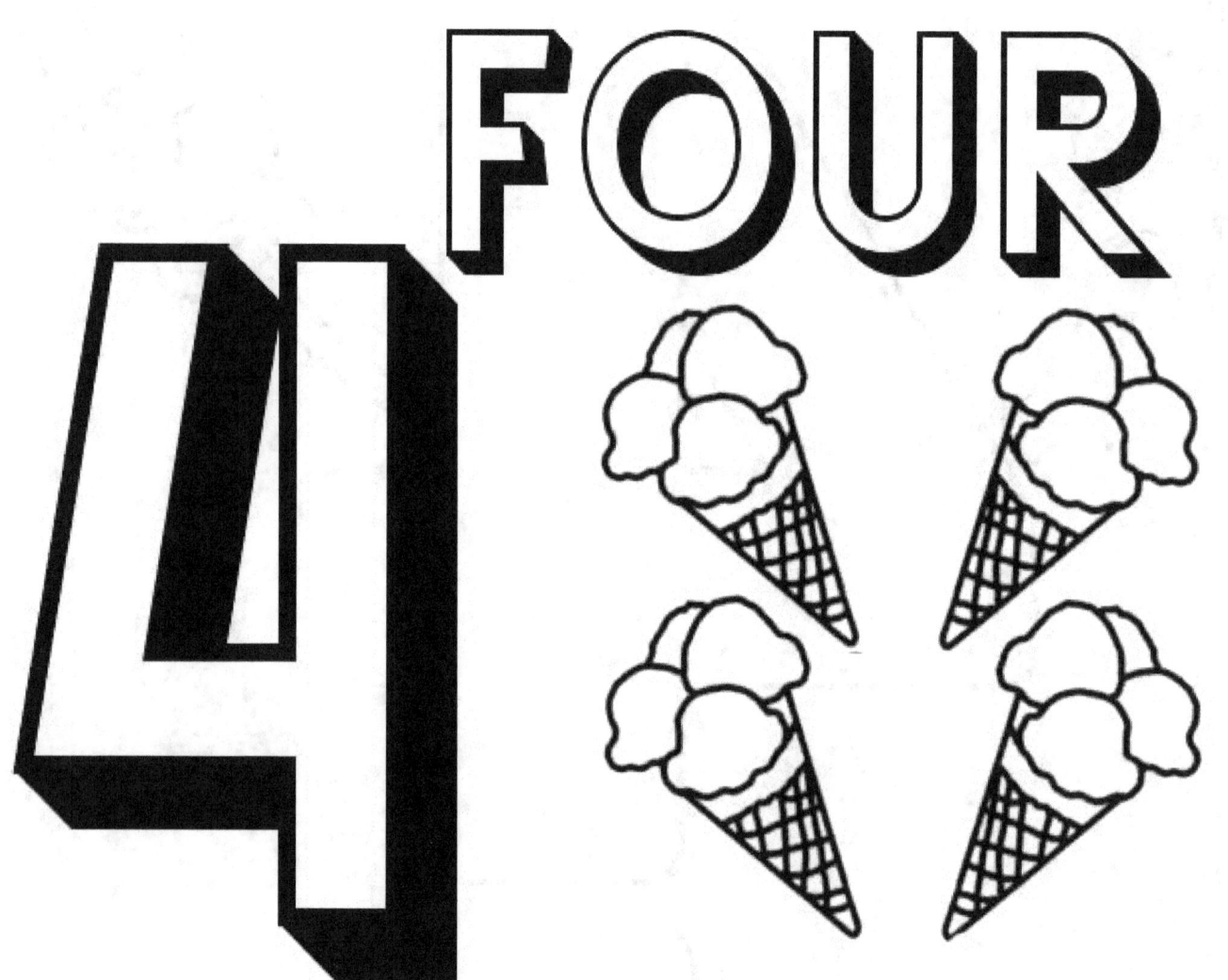

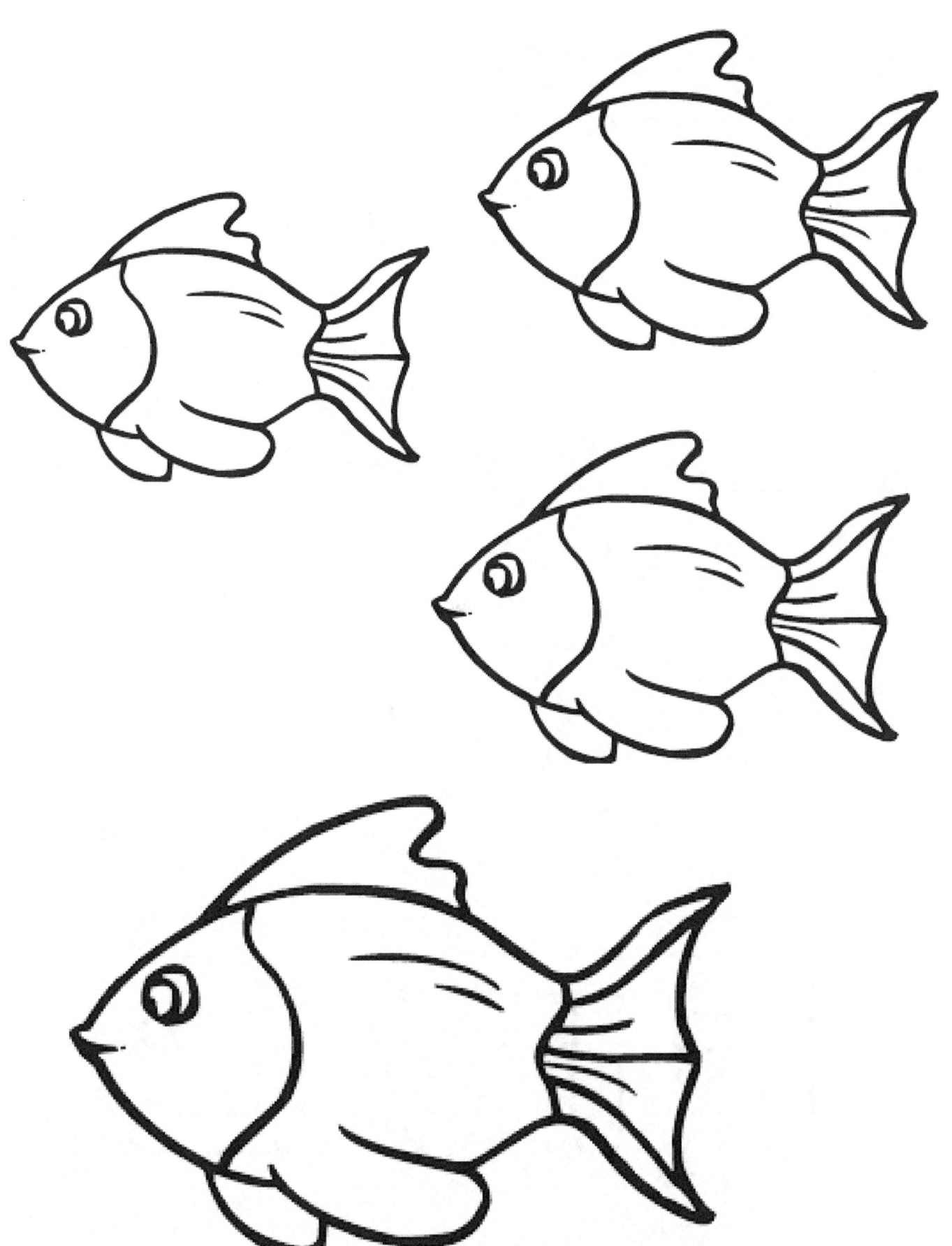

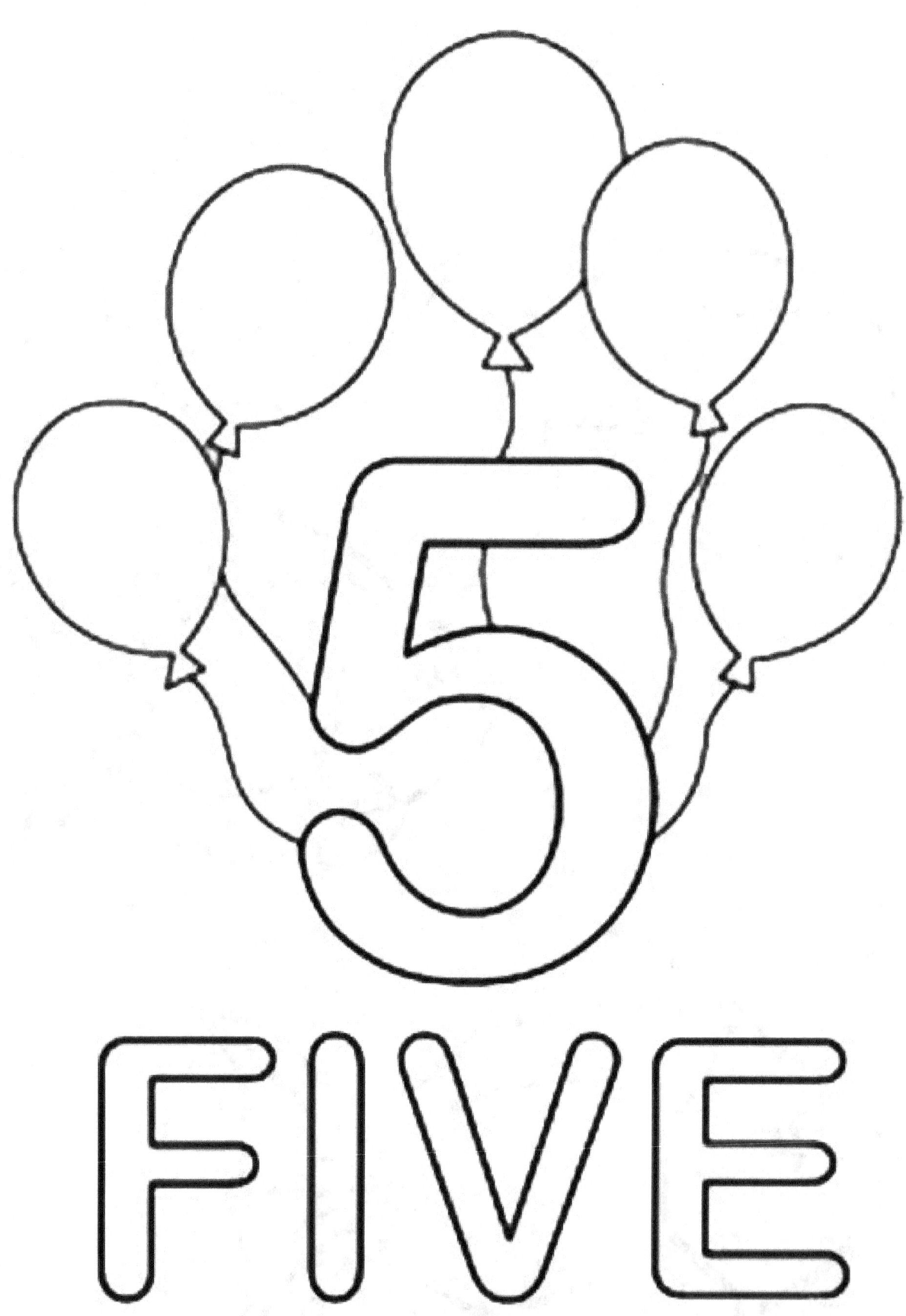

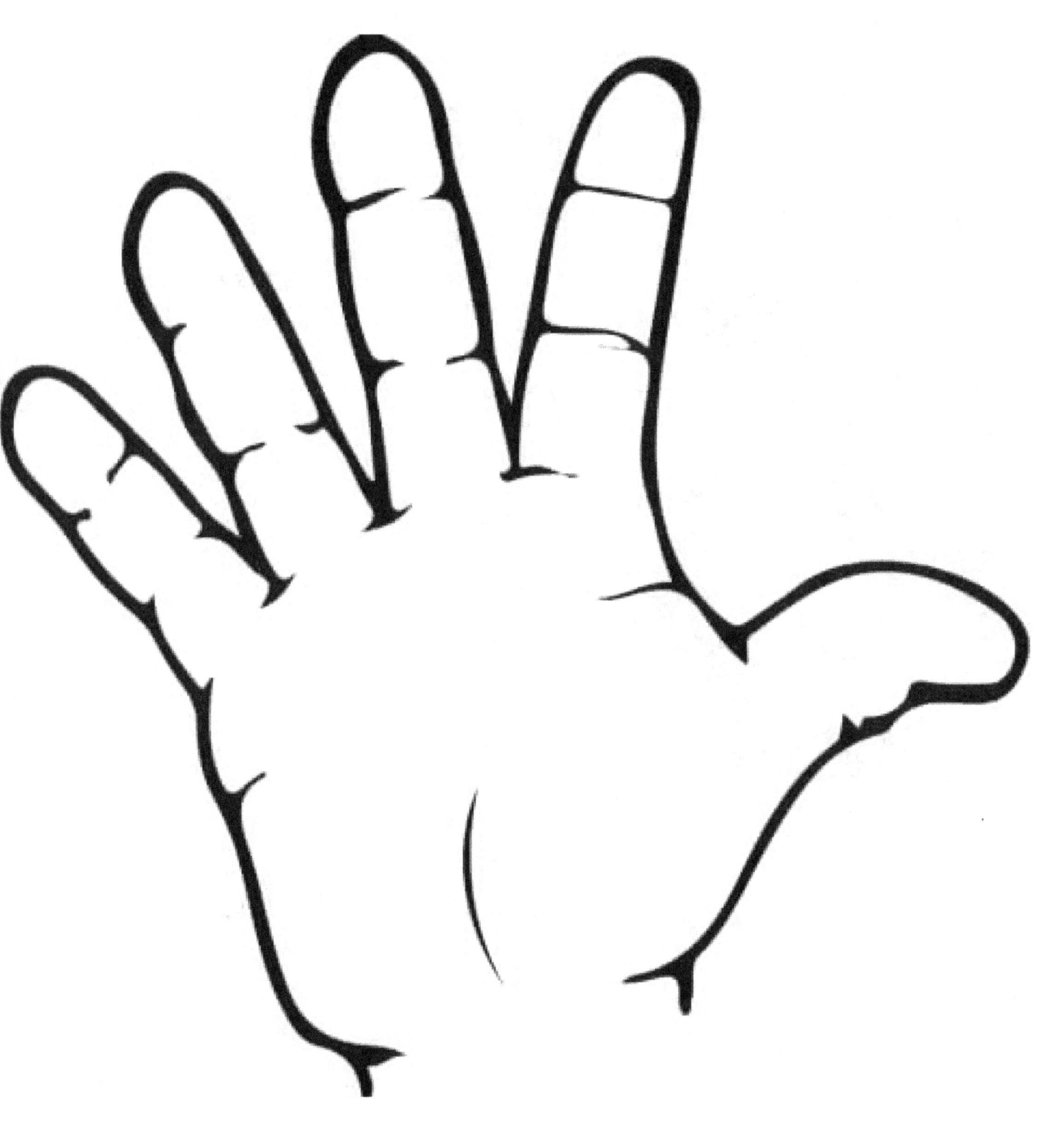

FIVE

5

FIVE EGGS

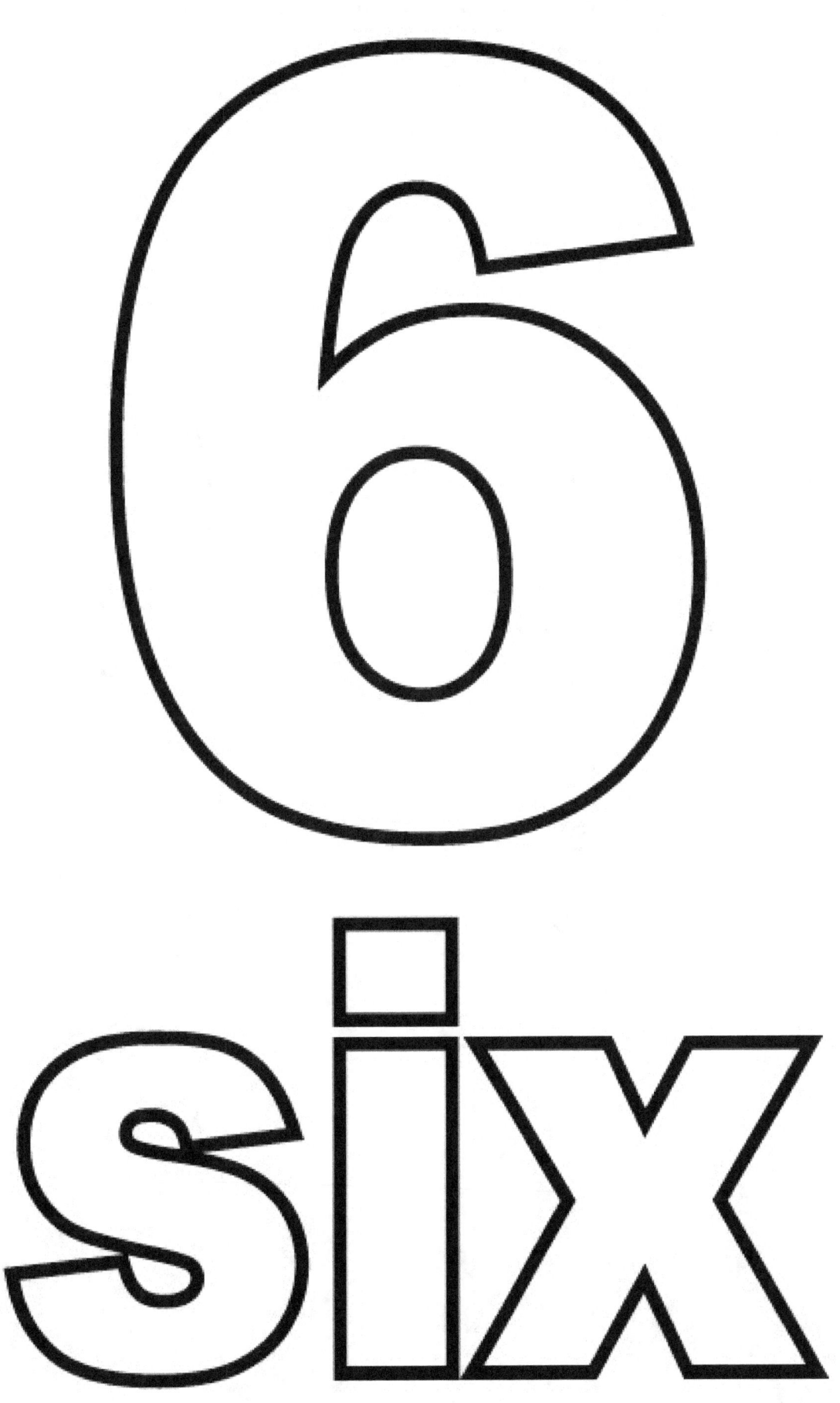

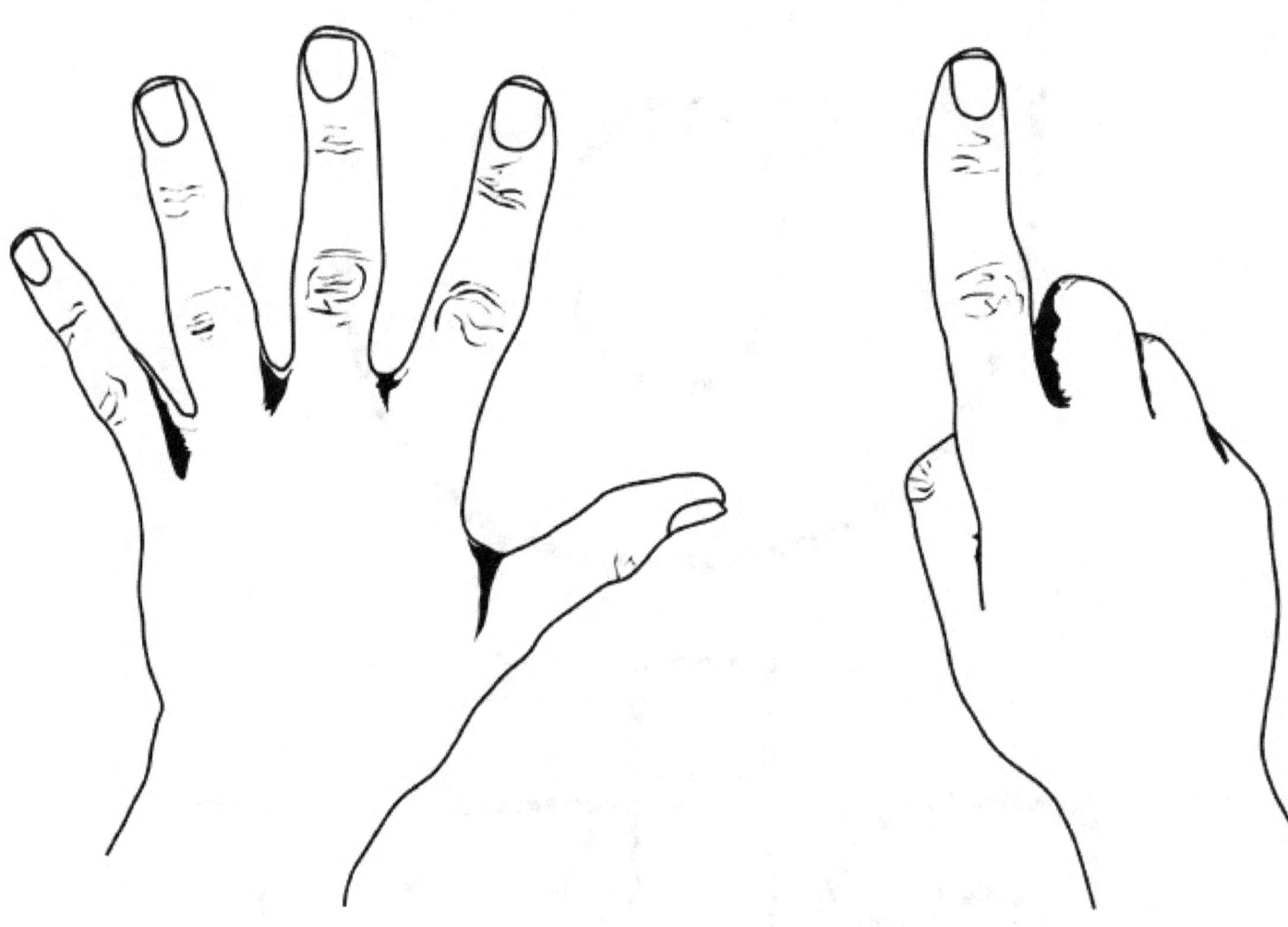

Tomato

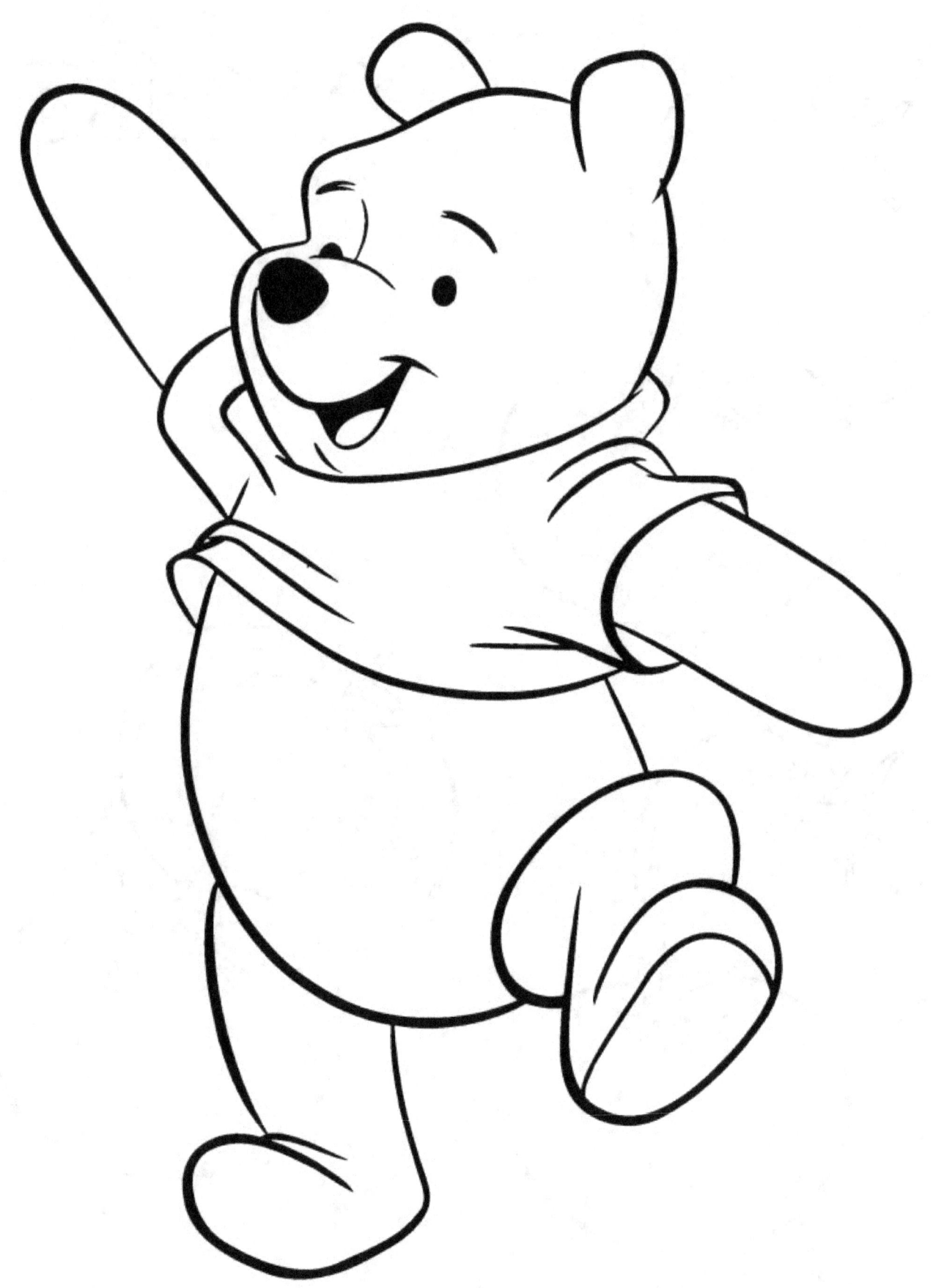

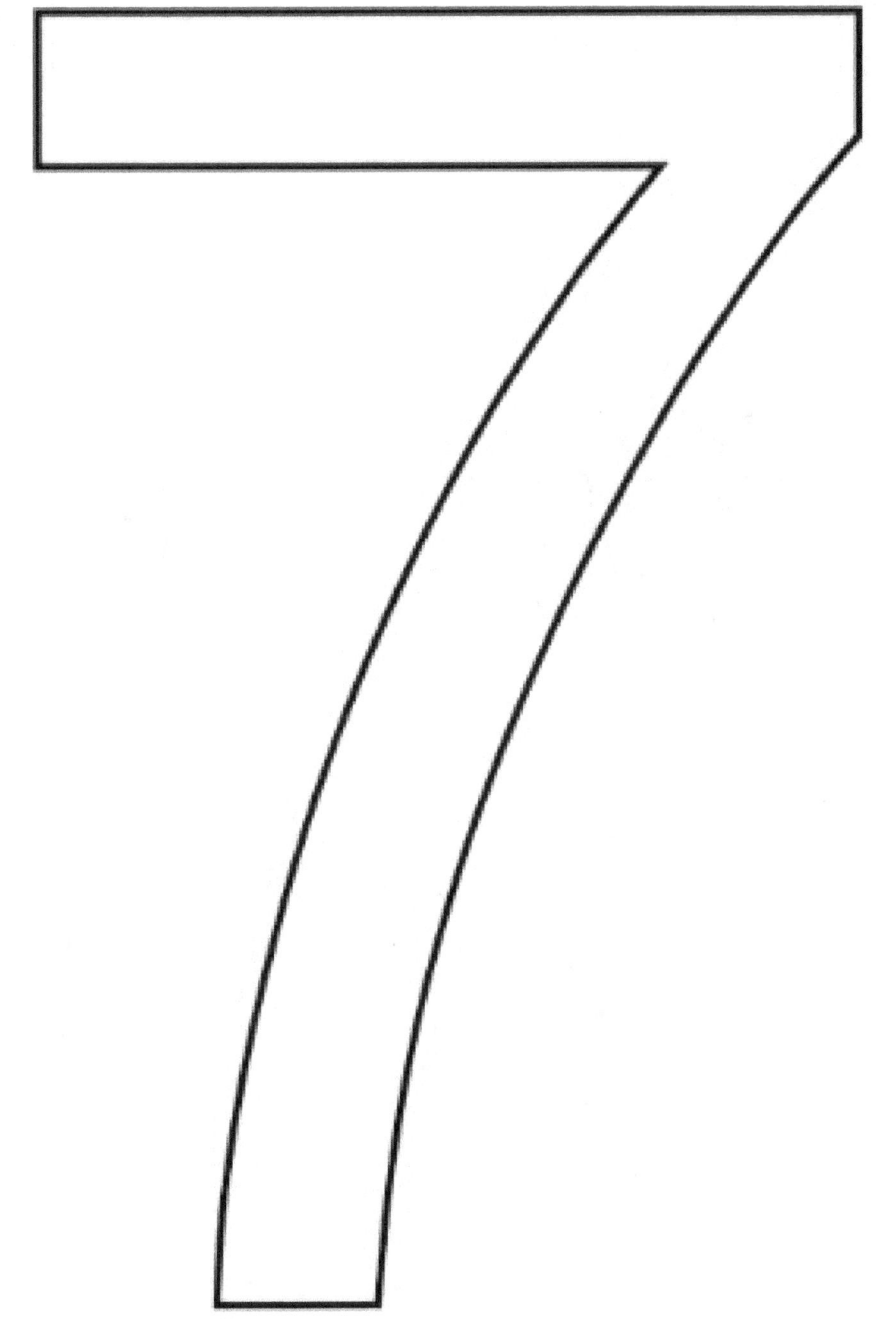

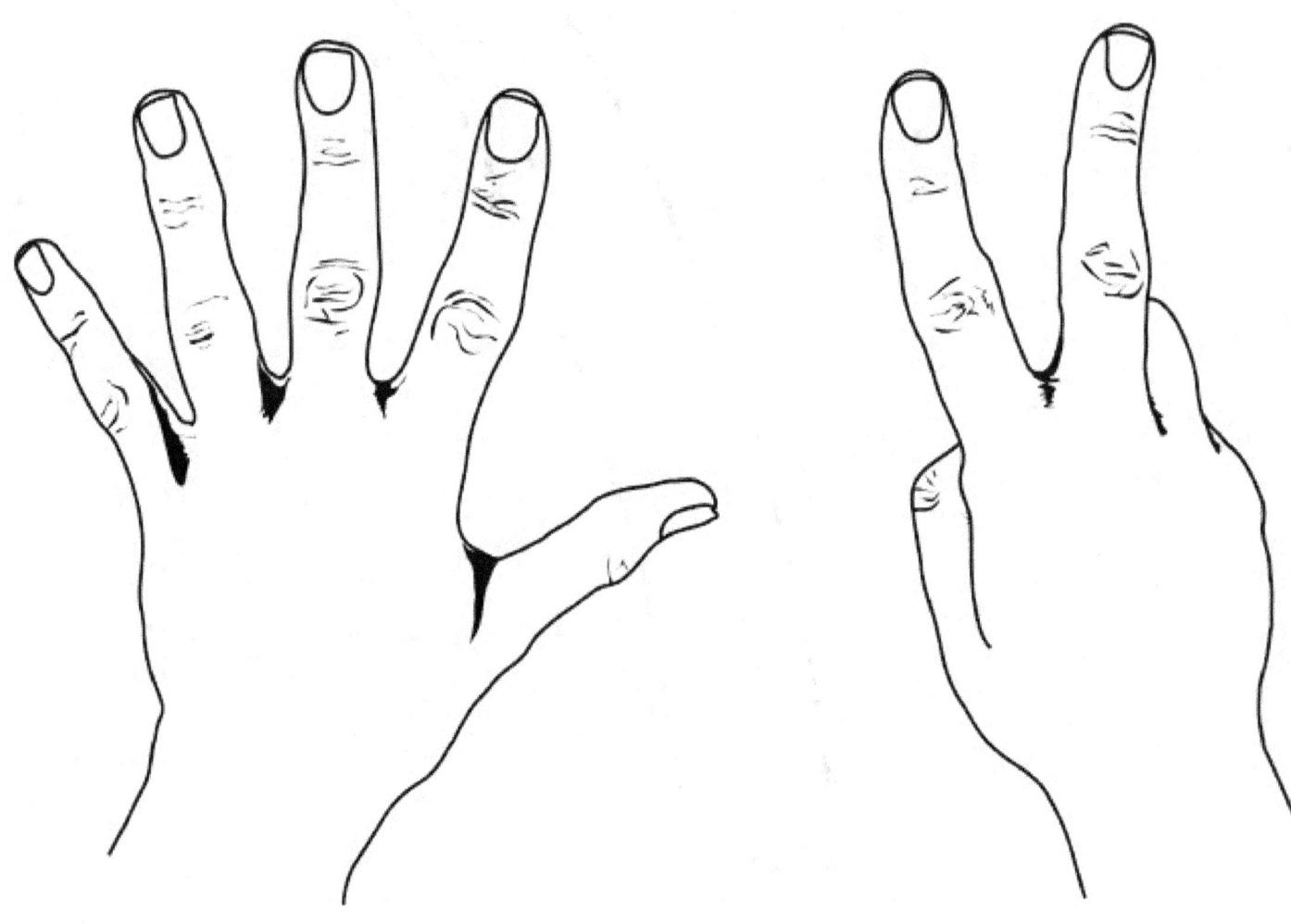

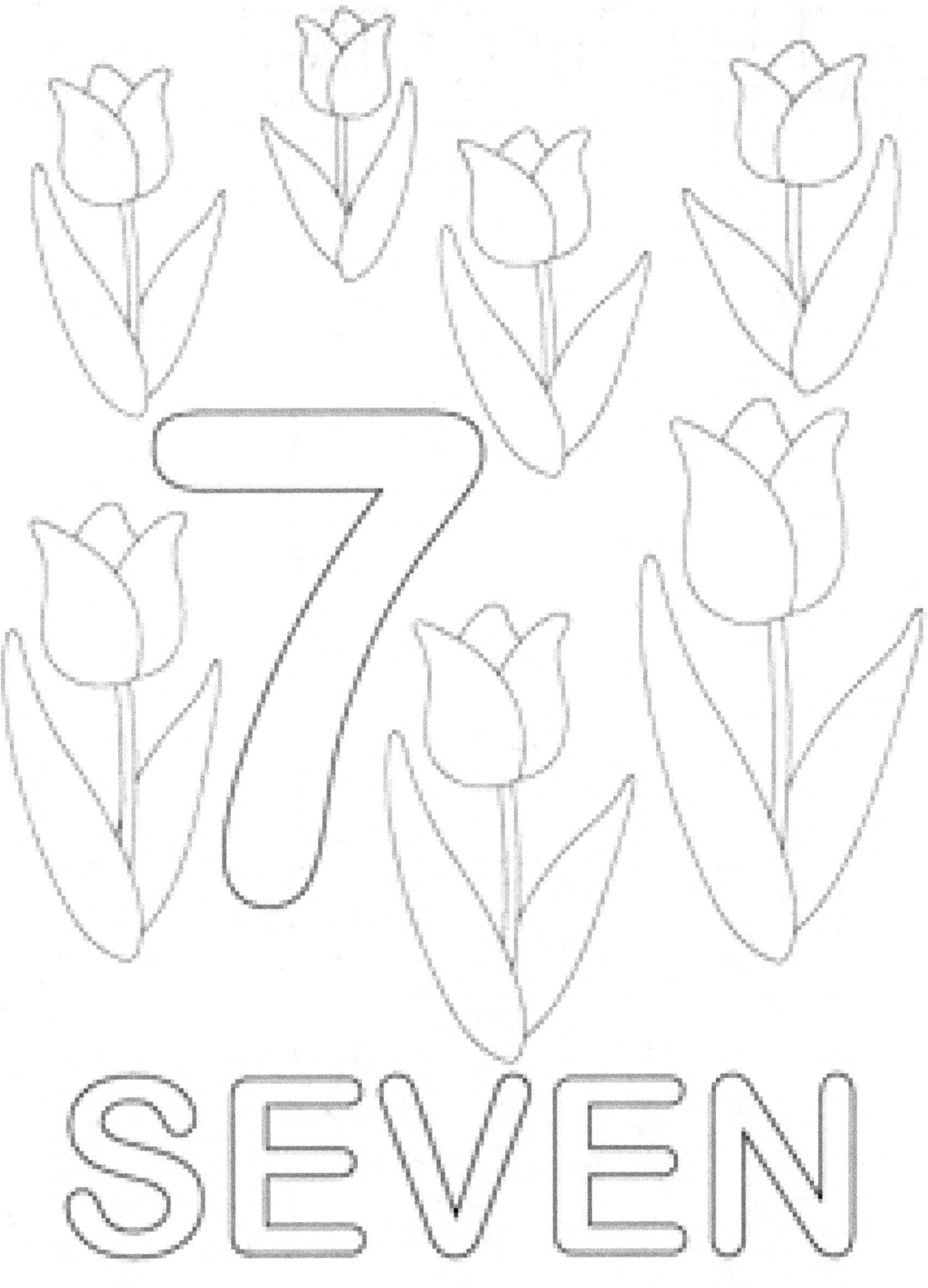

AUBERGINE

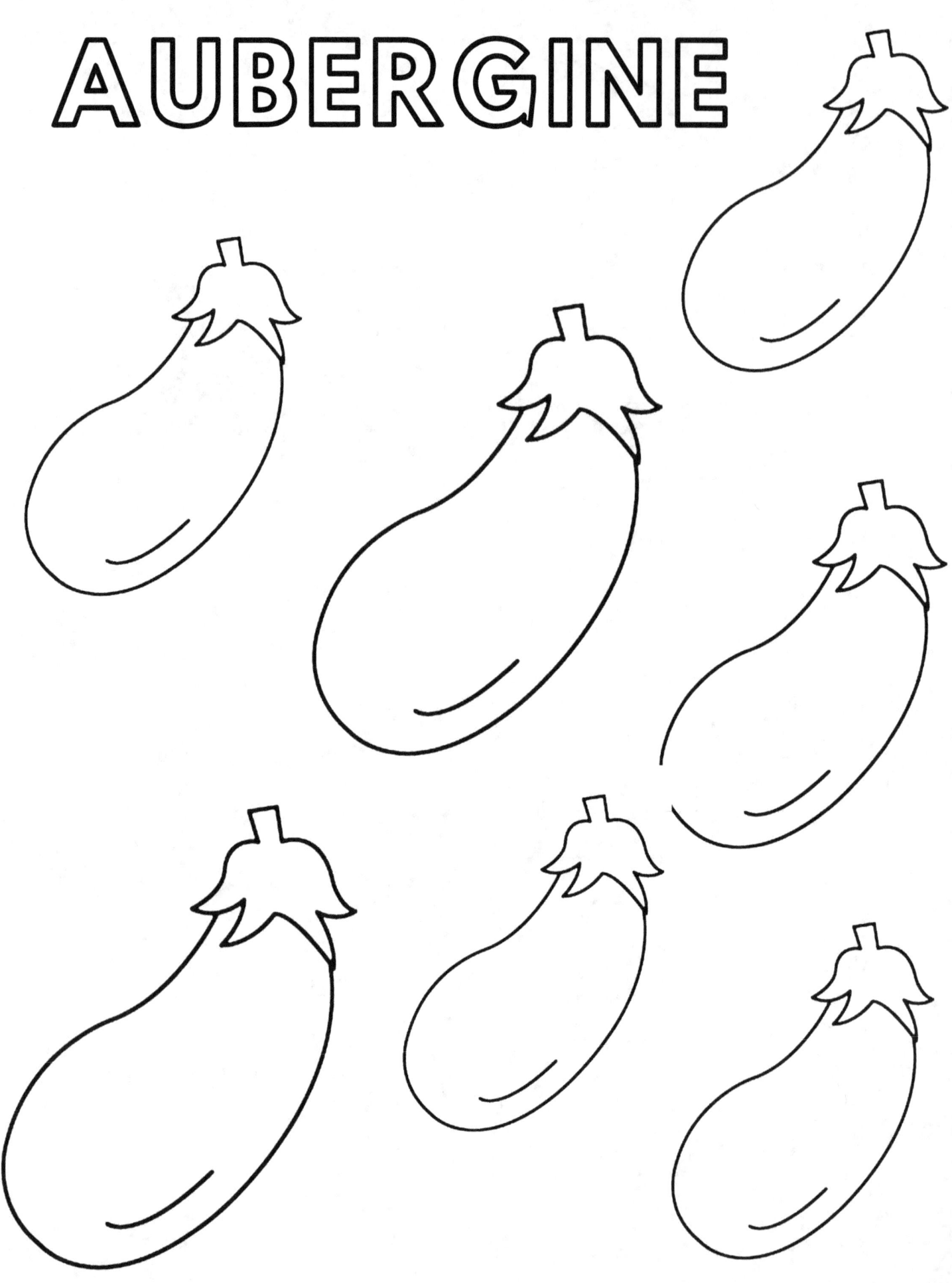

eight

8

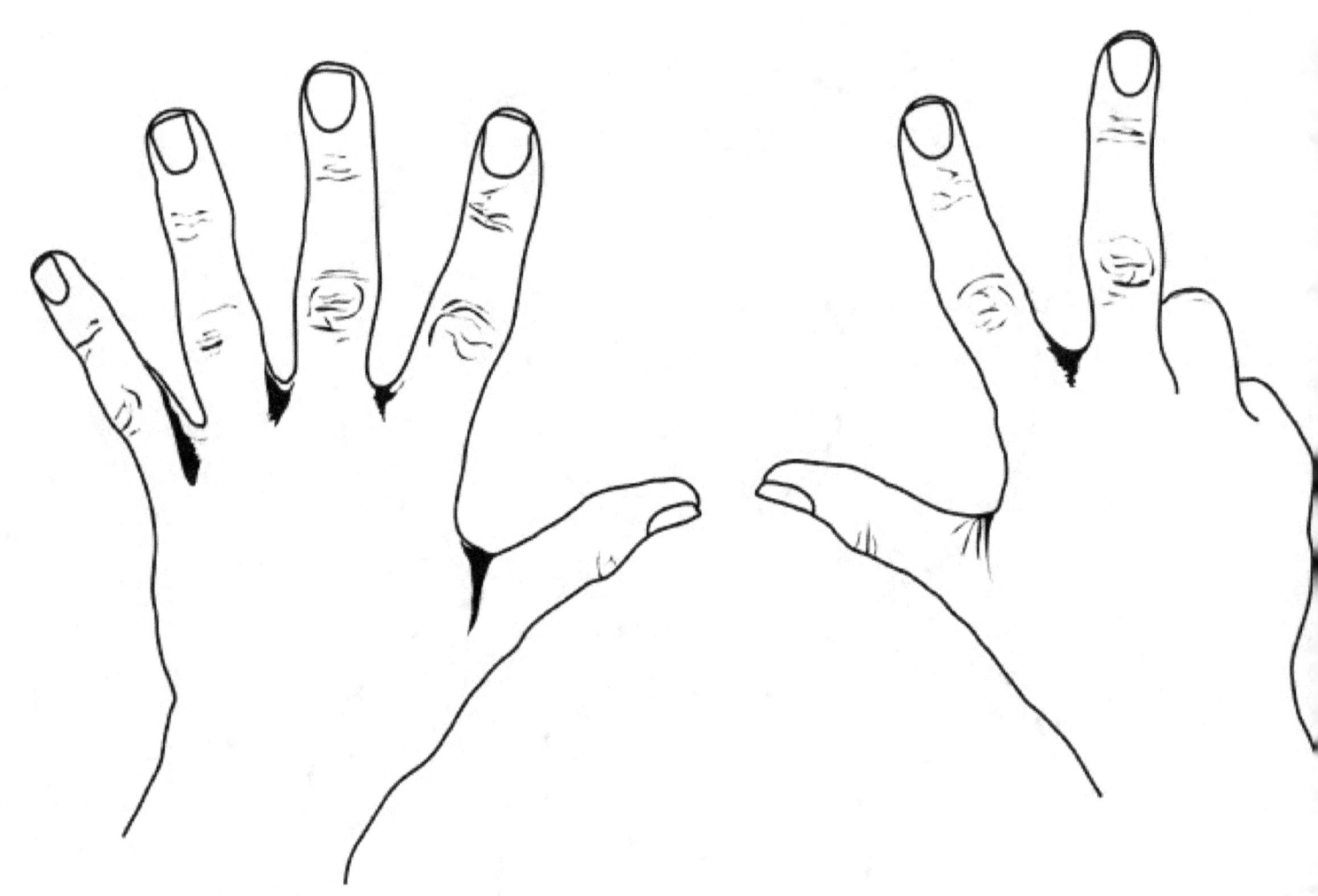

EIGHT

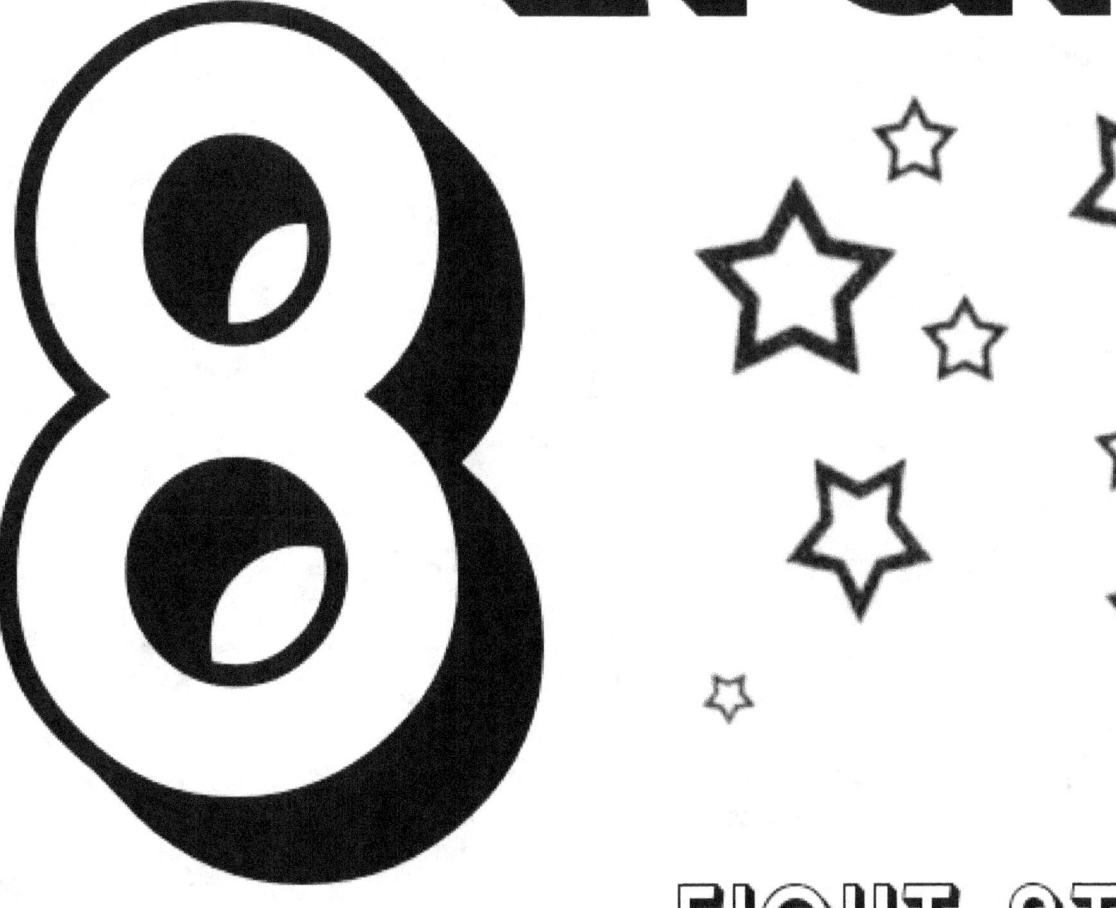

EIGHT STARS

FISH

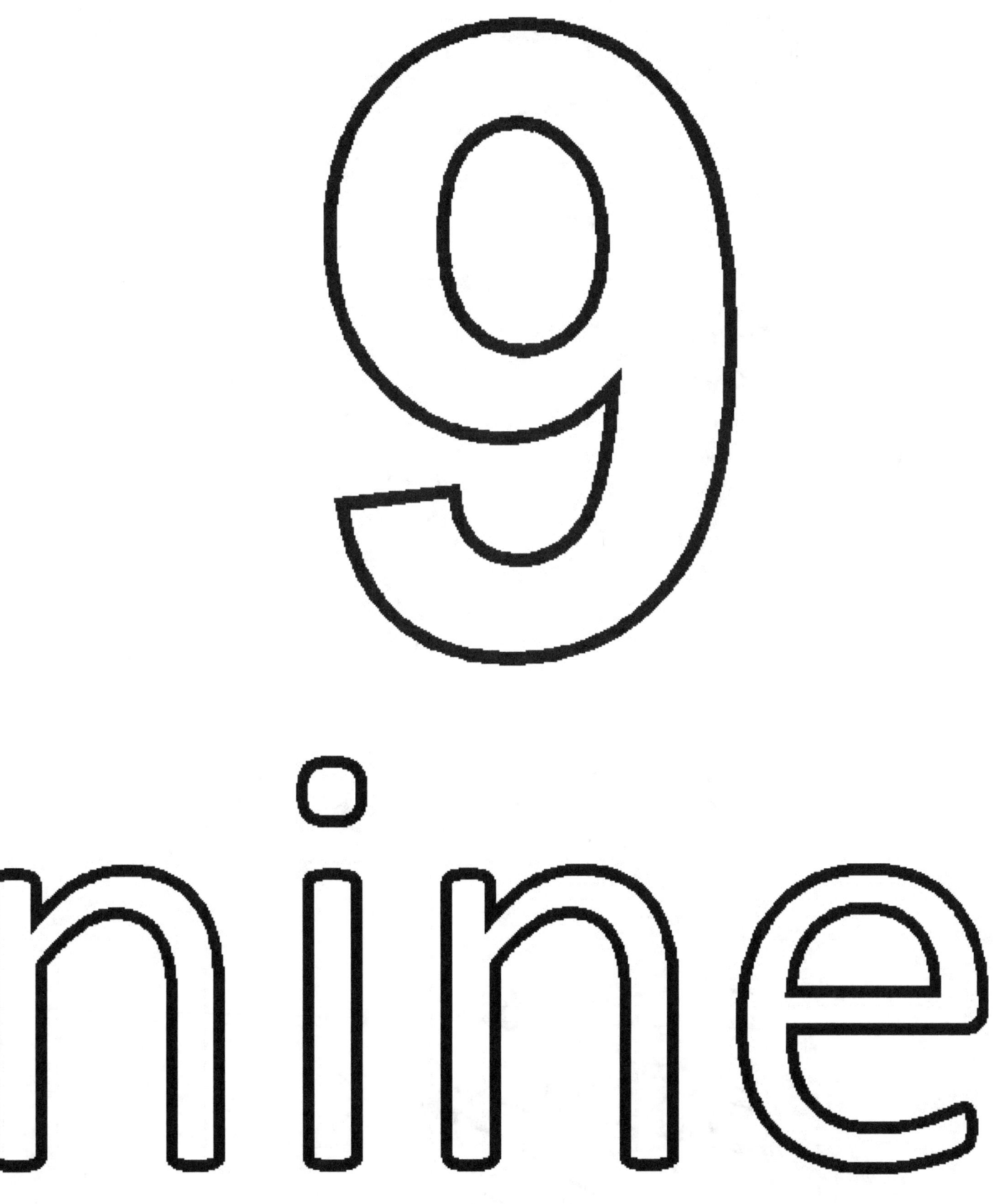

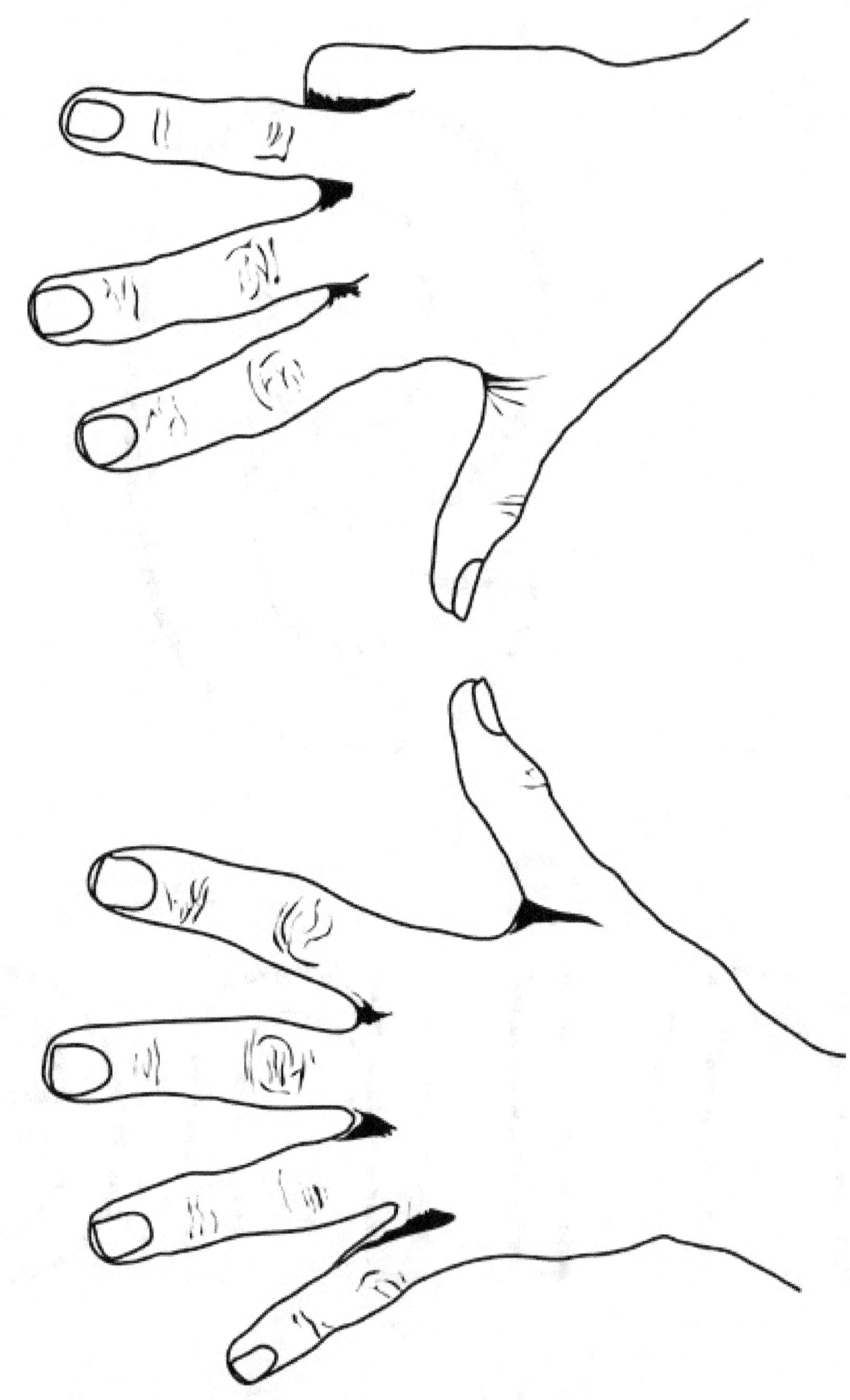

STRAWBERRIES

9

NINE

NINE APPLES

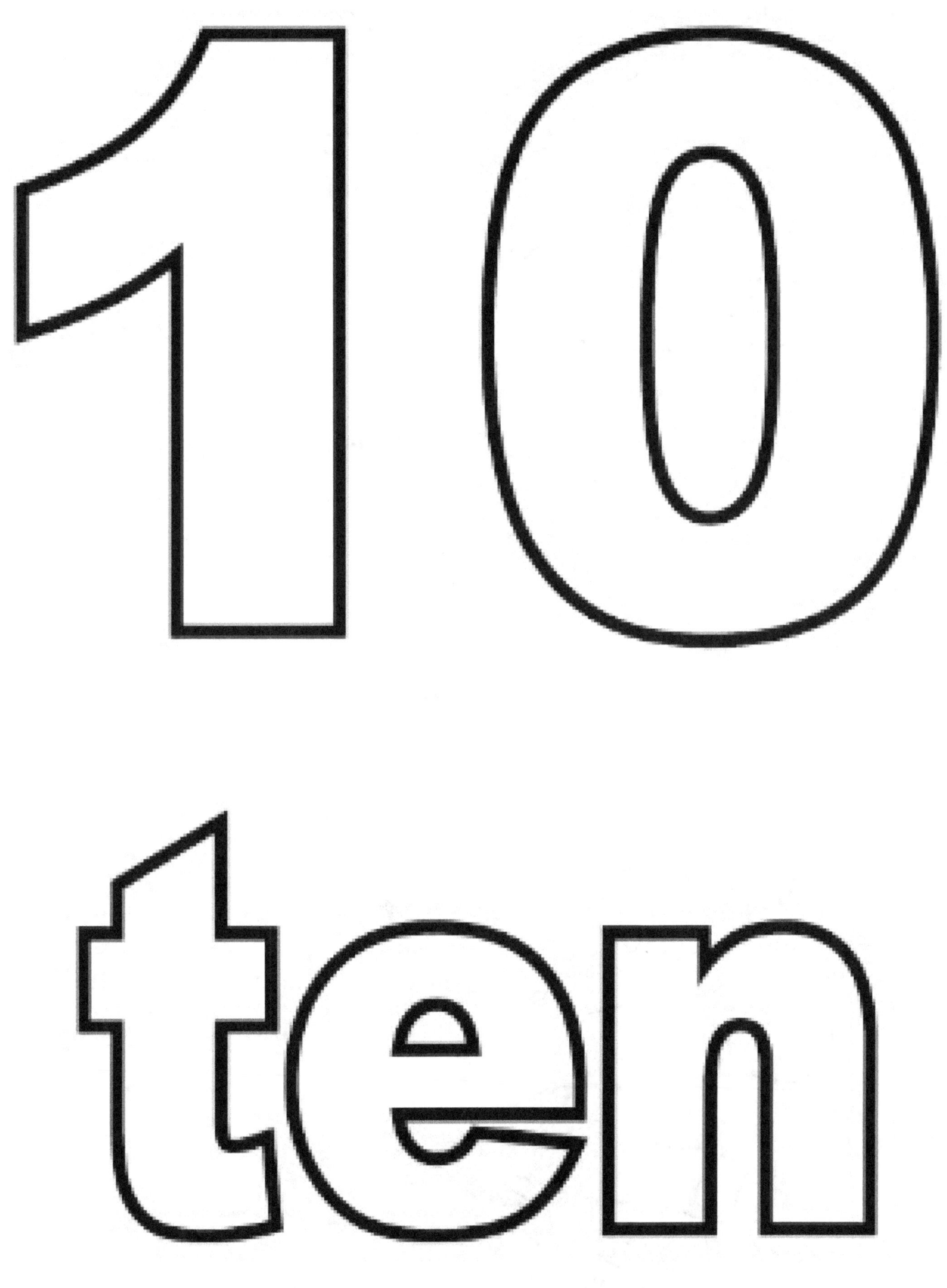

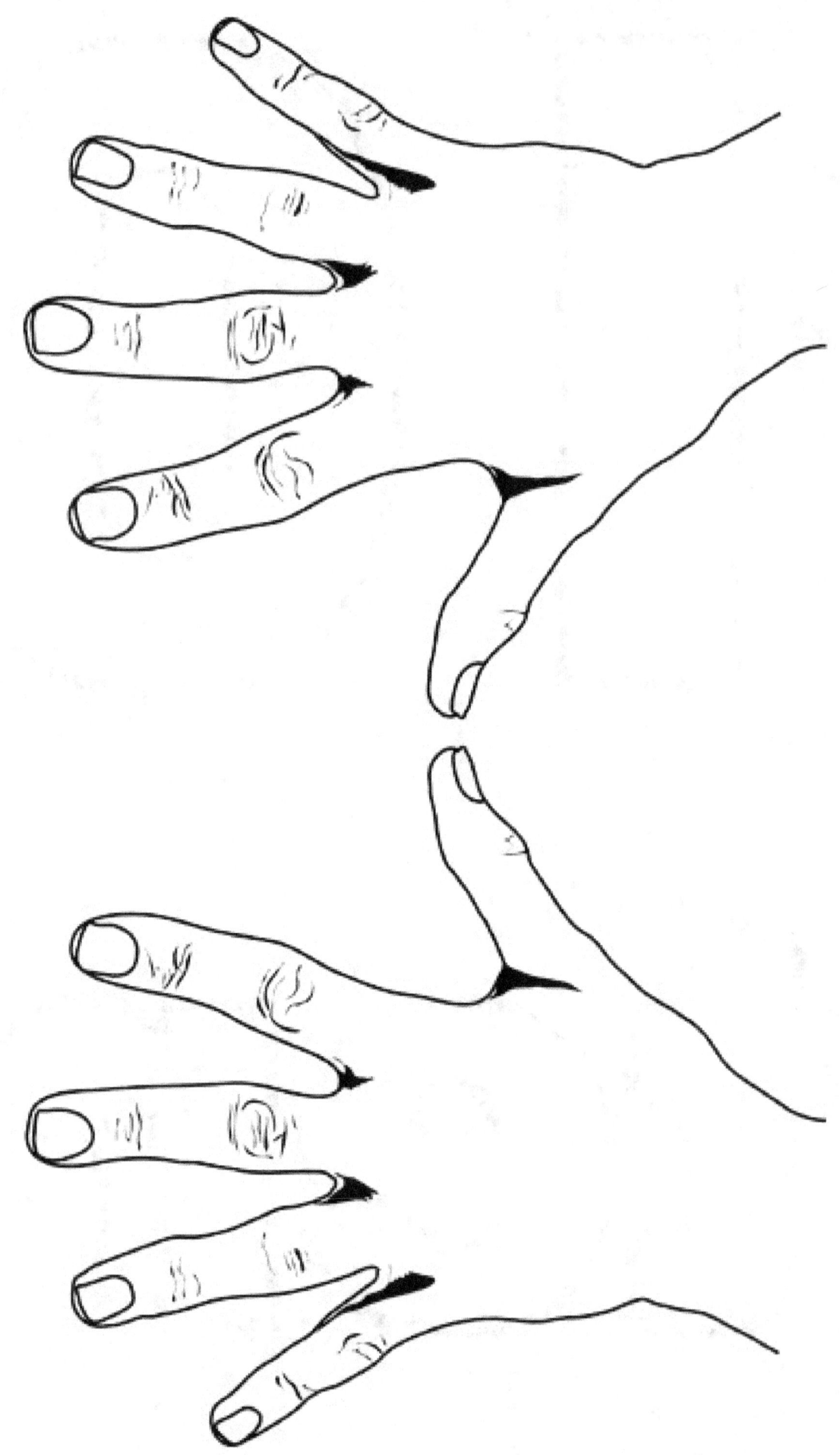

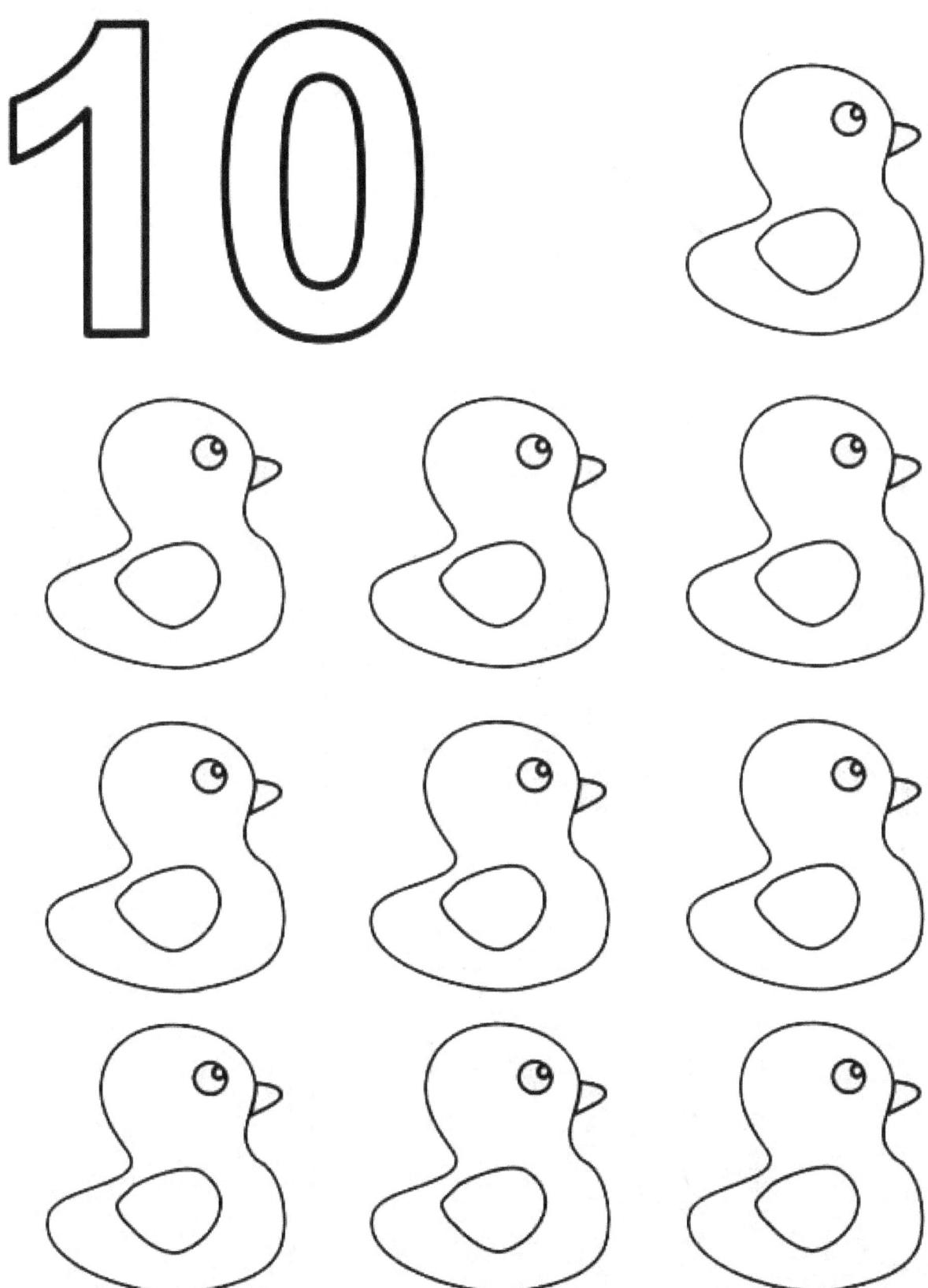

1 2 3 4

5 6 7 8

9 10

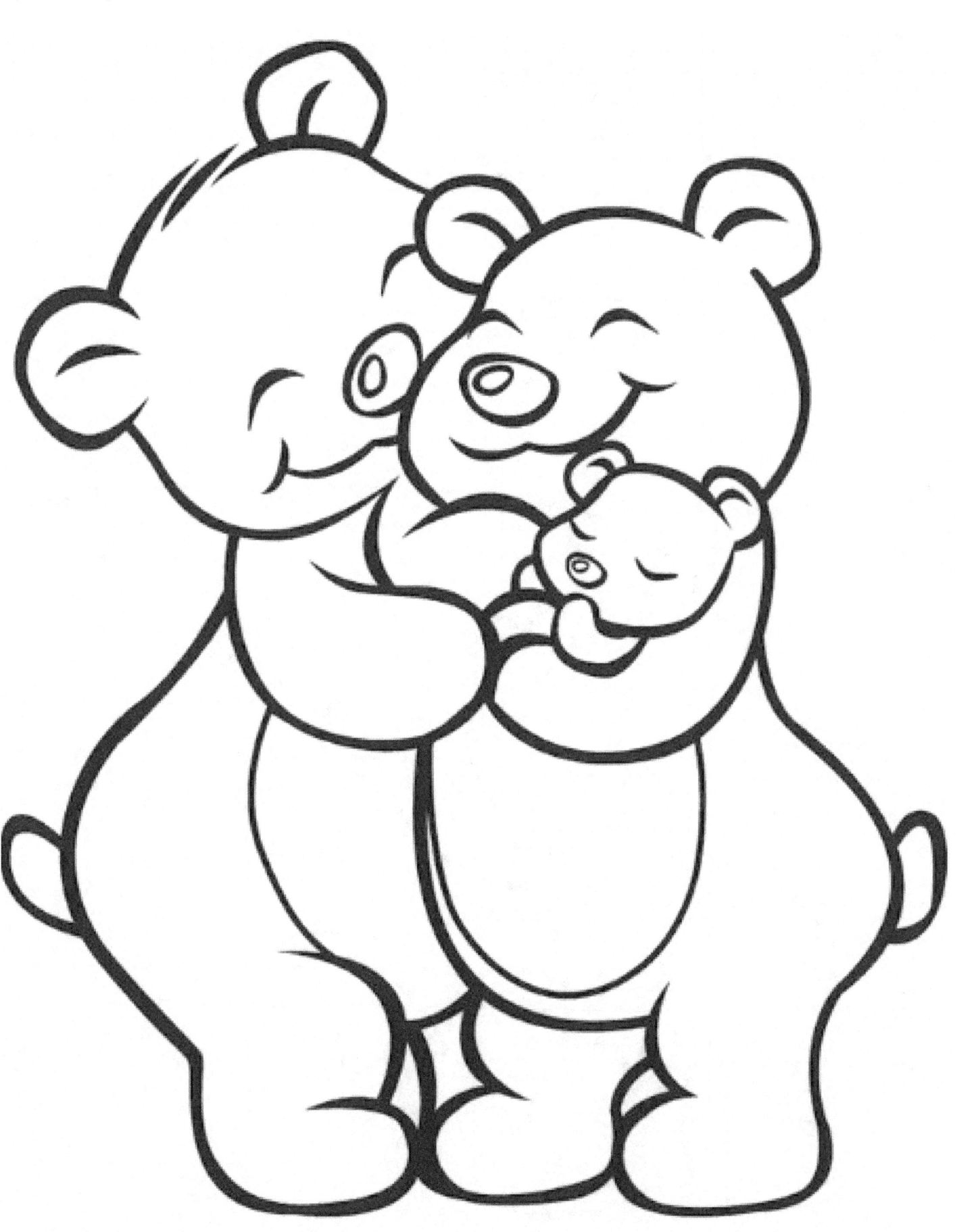

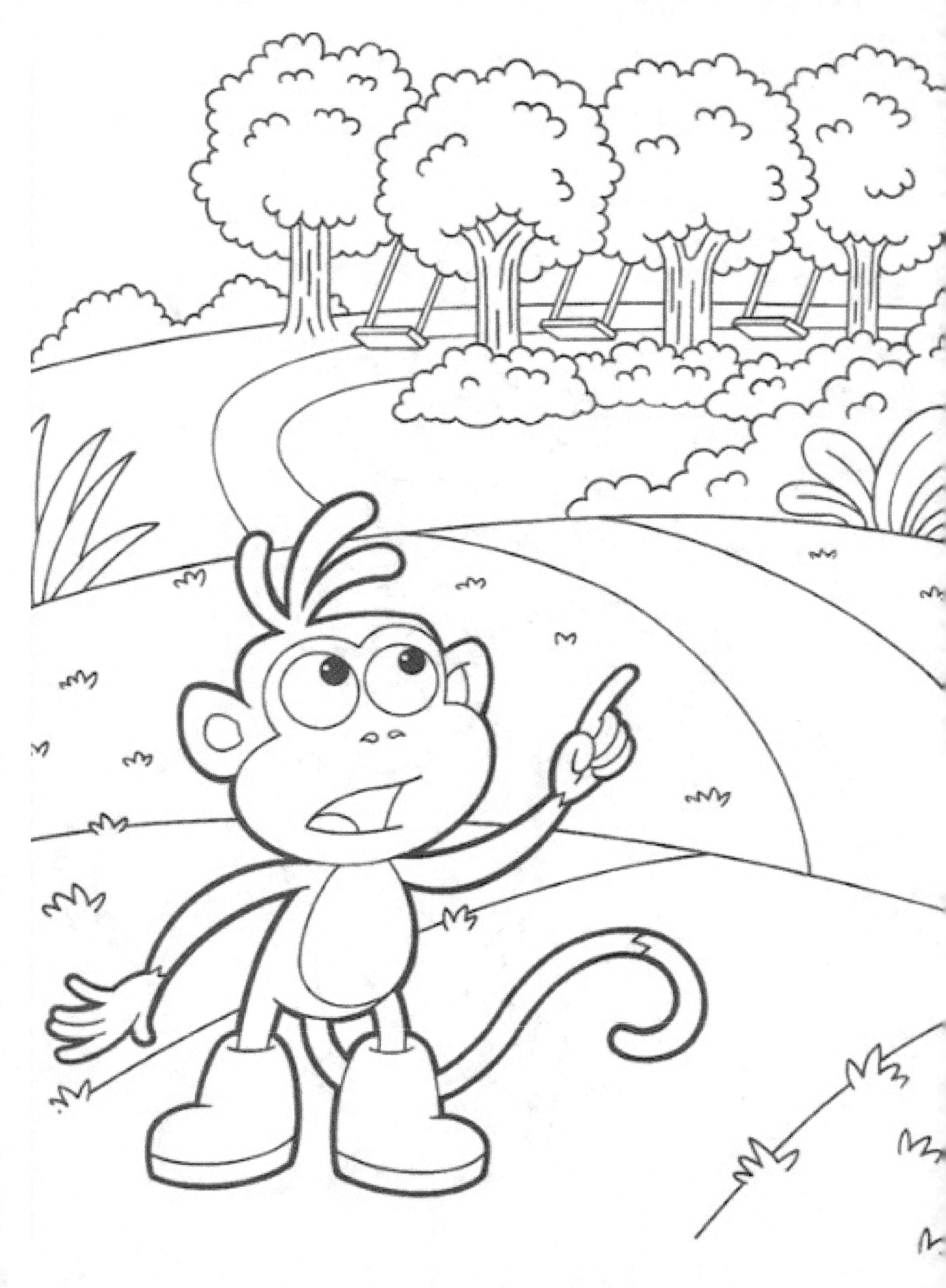